ONE AVERAGE DAY

ONE AVERAGE DAY

OREGON PROJECT DAYSHOOT PHOTOGRAPHS / 15 JULY 1983

WESTERN IMPRINTS
THE PRESS OF THE OREGON HISTORICAL SOCIETY
1984

Cover: The photographs on the cover of this publication are included in the main body of the collection (as numbered) and were taken by Ross Hamilton (top left [No. 203]), Beth Campbell (top right [No. 98]), Claudia J. Howell (center [No. 138]), Randy Wood (center right [No. 161]), Betty Udesen (bottom left [No. 122]), Dale Swanson (bottom center [No. 140]) and Dan Bates (bottom right [No. 79]).

Quotations from *Half a Truth is Better Than None,* by John A. Kouwenhoven, is by permission of the University of Chicago Press, and copyrighted by the University of Chicago Press, 1982.

One Average Day was designed and produced by Western Imprints, The Press of the Oregon Historical Society.

Main entry under title:
One average day.
    "Oregon Project Dayshoot photographs."
    1. Oregon—Description and travel—1981—   —Views.   2. Oregon—Social life and customs—Pictorial works.   I. Oregon Historical Society
F877.062 1984   979.5'043   84-2328
ISBN 0-87595-132-5
ISBN 0-87595-133-3 (pbk.)

Printed in the United States of America

CONTENTS

PREFACE

This book is the result of a collaboration among photojournalists and freelance photographers to visually document a day in the life of Oregon, and is a distillation of photographs taken during Project Dayshoot, on 15 July 1983. It is easily one of the most ambitious photojournalistic projects accomplished in Oregon. The collective effort behind Project Dayshoot grew out of a 1982 group exhibit by nearly three dozen Portland-area newspaper photographers.

In February of 1983, a month before the close of a second annual exhibit, a small group of participants met at the residence of Michael Lloyd, staff photographer for the *Oregonian,* to discuss prospects for the year ahead.

The group had been invited by Robert A. Stark, Oregon Historical Society museums administrator, to produce an exhibit in the early spring of 1984 for the Oregon Historical Center's 3,700-square-foot main floor gallery. A proviso was added that whatever was exhibited would be donated to the Photograph Library of the Society. This left the group faced with the challenge of filling one of the finest galleries in the Pacific Northwest with "something photojournalistic."

The notion of attempting a one-day project was first proposed as a special display within the main exhibit. But the appeal of gambling the entire gallery display on one day's work began to grow quickly. Such a one-day project had been accomplished in Australia (with "one hundred of the world's leading photojournalists" and a "million-dollar budget"), and had resulted in a stunning, showcase book, *A Day in the Life of Australia.* However, for the Oregon group there was no budget and no prospect of doing a book at the time.

Debate centered upon whether enough photographers from around the state would participate to make the venture worthwhile, or whether the project should be confined to the Portland area.

As it had supported the development of earlier photographic exhibits, the Oregon Newspaper Publishers Association (ONPA) offered its WATS line to query nearly every newspaper in Oregon with staff photographers. Enthusiasm expressed around the state was almost unanimous, and the decision was made to attempt a one-day coverage for the entire state. Support also came from the National Press Photographers Association (NPPA).

Lloyd's residence became headquarters for weekly meetings from March through June (two general meetings were held during this time, one in Salem under the direction of Mike Williams and one in Corvallis

with Jim Folts). Lloyd's living room wall soon sported a huge map of Oregon. The state was quartered, with each section assigned directors responsible for researching that area, planning coverage and recruiting photographers.

The offer to each photographer was simple. On the chosen day, the participant would cover his or her own area, primarily in black-and-white, with each photographer assuming expenses. Two weeks following that date, all participants would submit prints (each accompanied by full information about the photograph), along with proofsheets of their entire shooting for the day.

Although all photographs submitted would become part of a permanent collection to be housed in the Society's Research Library, only a limited number of images could be selected from submissions for the 1984 exhibit. It was stressed to the individual photographers that there was no guarantee their work would be chosen for display.

Before the end of March, David Hoffman, regional representative for Ilford, Inc., heard of the project and stepped in with an offer by his company to donate its best photographic paper for printing the exhibit. With the single major expense of the project resolved, it was felt a modest success was assured.

Then the Oregon Historical Society made an additional commitment to the project.

In a letter dated 1 April 1983, Bruce Taylor Hamilton, executive editor, Western Imprints, The Press of the Oregon Historical Society, expressed interest in producing a book from Project Dayshoot. In spite of the "tough reality" of the production schedule at Western Imprints, he wanted to issue the book in conjunction with the opening of the exhibit. The proposed book would be more than a catalog of the exhibit, but a substantial enterprise in its own right.

Needless to say, the prospect of a book, which would preserve the project, greatly enhanced photojournalists' participation. Hamilton himself proved invaluable as a driving force for focusing organizational efforts.

By the middle of May, the state map on Lloyd's living room wall bristled with stick-on tabs, each denoting photographers and subjects. About 65 photographers were confirmed as participants.

The date of coverage was set for Friday, 15 July 1983. A Friday was chosen to combine elements of the work week with the beginning of weekend recreation, and 15 July was selected because it was far enough away from any major holiday to better represent daily life in Oregon.

Governor Victor Atiyeh proclaimed 15 July as "Oregon Photojournalism Day" in recognition of the contributions the state's photojournalists would be making.

The day itself seemed to come and go very quickly, leaving some surprises as well as disappointments. A few key people withdrew from participation at the last minute, due to other demands. Some volunteers sprang up unknown to the organizers of the project until their prints arrived two weeks later.

The day had its ironies.

It turned out to be the birthday of the *Springfield News* staff photographer, Betty Udesen. She spent nearly 24 hours shooting, and she came up with the third highest number of images selected for the book.

Nearby, in a Springfield hospital, the director of photography for the *Eugene Register-Guard,* Charlie Nye, documented his wife giving birth to their daughter, Abby Ruth Nye, before going out and shooting more coverage for the project.

The state's only nuclear plant was opened to one photographer while another roamed through the state's penitentiary, both virtually without restriction. Ironically, another photographer was forbidden to take any pictures inside a Portland shopping mall, despite advance inquiry and a letter of introduction from the Oregon Historical Society. And, in spite of his own ambitious plans for the day, Lloyd was sent by his newspaper to the state capitol to cover the end of the second-longest legislative session in state history.

All in all, 15 July was not an extraordinary day. It was simply one day examined by a diverse and talented group of photojournalists doing essentially what they do every workingday, watching their world through a 35mm window.

On the first weekend in August, the directors for the project (along with a few volunteers) gathered at the offices of the Oregon Historical Society's publishing department, Western Imprints, to sort the submitted photographs. Project Dayshoot's ambitious effort had paid off in nearly 2,000 images contributed by more than 90 photographers.

The project itself was concluded that weekend. What was left to the photograph editors was the refining of a wonderful mosaic into a coherent portrait of 15 July 1983.

But, had 14 July or 16 July—or 23 September—been chosen for coverage, the kaleidoscope of images would have shifted and these same photographers would have produced an entirely different collection.

Think about that three hundred and sixty four or five times....

On behalf of the project directors,

Michal Thompson
Staff photographer
Hillsboro Argus

Project co-directors-at-large: Michael Lloyd, Michal Thompson

Northwest section directors: Ross Hamilton, Michal Thompson

Northeast section directors: Steve Nehl, David Weintraub

Southeast section directors: Gregory J. Lawler, Michael Lloyd

Southwest section directors: Cathy Cheney, J. L. Clark

PARTICIPANTS

Steve Aamodt
Milwaukie

Dail Maxine Adams
Oregon Military Dept.
of Public Affairs
Salem

Tom Ballard
News-Register
McMinnville

Dan Bastian
Bend

Dan Bates
Register-Guard
Eugene

Cheryl K. Blankenship
Gresham

Steve Bloch
Portland

Marv Bondarowicz
Portland

Lori Borgman-Nye
Register-Guard
Eugene

Alan Borrud
Lake Oswego Review

John Bragg
Gazette-Times
Corvallis

Christopher Briscoe
Ashland

Beth Campbell
Columbian
Vancouver, Washington

Jill A. Cannefax
Dayton

Rae Carey
RFD Publications
Portland

Cathy Cheney
Willamette Week
Portland

Dan Clark
La Grande

J. L. Clark
Lake Oswego

Kevin Clark
Register-Guard
Eugene

Averie Cohen
Oakland, California

S. John Collins
Democrat-Herald
Baker

Paul V. Colvin
Portland

Ron Cooper
Salem

Lyle Cox
Bulletin
Bend

Maury Dahlen
Portland

Joel Davis
Oregonian
Portland

Thomas Davis
Bend

Steve Dipaola
Hillsboro

Wayne Eastburn
Register-Guard
Eugene

Robert Ellis
Oregonian
Portland

Paul Engstrom
Oregonian
Portland

David Falconer
Portland

Terry Farris
Times Publications
Tigard

C. Bruce Forster
Portland

Shan Gordon
Times Publications
Tigard

Christie Gray
Gaston

Barbara F. Gundle
Portland

Dee Ann Hall
Salem

Ross Hamilton
Oregonian
Portland

Michael Hinsdale
Astoria

Larry K. Hoffman
Daily Argus Observer
Ontario

Don Hovell
Times Publications
Tigard

Claudia J. Howell
Portland

Bill Hunter
Democrat-Herald
Albany

Rich Iwasaki
Portland

Robert Jaffe
Jacksonville

Roger Jensen
Oregonian
Portland

Tim Jewett
Oregonian
Portland

Dean J. Koepfler
Statesman-Journal
Salem

Diane Kulpinski
Bulletin
Bend

Gregory J. Lawler
Portland

Michael Lloyd
Oregonian
Portland

Renée McKoy
Monmouth

Vanessa McVay
Oakridge

John Maher
Portland

Robert Mixon
Portland

Steve Nehl
Oregonian
Portland

David Nishitani
Corvallis

Charlie Nye
Register-Guard
Eugene

Dana Olsen
Oregonian
Portland

Katherine Palmer
Tillamook

Michael Parker
Portland

Geoff Parks
Portland

Greg Paul
Hood River

Robert Pennell
East Oregonian
Pendleton

Bryan F. Peterson
Gaston

Randy L. Rasmussen
Oregonian
Portland

Karen Rathe
Tillamook

Don Ratliff
Madras

Bill Rhodes
Madras

Susan A. Romanitis
St. Johns Review
Portland

Ken Selland
Newport

Marsha A. Shewczyk
Warm Springs

Keith D. Skelton
Portland

Bruce Smith
Creswell

McLaren Stinchfield
Times-Journal
Condon

Lisa A. Stone
Portland

Cynthia D. Stowell
Portland

Dave Swan
Bend

Dale Swanson
Oregonian
Portland

Jim Thompson
Times Publications
Tigard

Michal Thompson
Hillsboro Argus

Bruce Thorson
Daily Tidings
Ashland

Tom Treick
Oregonian
Portland

Betty Udesen
Springfield News

Ed Vidinghoff
Vancouver, Washington

Mary Volm
Portland

Bill Wagner
Daily Astorian

Tom Warren
Corvallis

David Weintraub
Portland

Brent Wojahn
Oregonian
Portland

Randy Wood
Oregonian
Portland

Photograph editors:	Cathy Cheney, Tim Jewett, Michael Lloyd
Writers: General Introduction:	Bruce Taylor Hamilton
Chapter introductions and captions:	Cynthia Doherty, Paul Pintarich, Bruce Taylor Hamilton and Stephanie A. Smith
Exhibit designers:	Barbara F. Gundle, Gregory J. Lawler, Michal Thompson
Chief printer for exhibition:	Gregory J. Lawler
Photographic paper for exhibition:	Ilford, Inc.
Audio-visual designer:	Ed Vidinghoff
Exhibition:	One Average Day: Oregon Project Dayshoot Photographs 15 July 1983 Oregon Historical Center, Portland 15 March-28 April 1984

INTRODUCTION

One Average Day. Take any day, and you find that it has its "average" qualities—that it is part of the continuum, without which no society can survive. Yet, each day is unique, as all days are.

This day, 15 July 1983, chosen to be so well recorded by Project Dayshoot and reproduced in this volume, *One Average Day,* was an average day unlike any other. On no other single day in Oregon's past has there been such a concerted effort to record the day's events, places and people, to record them visually, and to have them recorded by persons whose profession is that of capturing the importance of an instant. It is doubtful that there will be any future Oregon day so well preserved in this manner.

Recognizing the significance of the undertaking, Governor Victor Atiyeh, in his proclamation designating 15 July 1983 as "Oregon Photojournalism Day," wrote that the photographers "will be documenting one average day in the history of Oregon." The governor's excellent choice of words gave this publication its title.

There is a danger in capturing an event or a day, that it will freeze our perception of a place or time. The nearly three hundred photographs reproduced in *One Average Day* are but an equal number of instants. In composite they record Oregon on 15 July 1983; a composite that can be filled by the imagination and knowledge of any and all who look at them closely. They do, therefore, offer a form of completeness.

However, each photograph records an instant in many processes. The baby whose birth is recorded on these pages is now much older—no more the seconds-old infant. Some of the persons pictured here have died, moved, changed jobs, or divorced; some may still be in the same place, but that place may constantly and irrevocably change.

Oregonians—Americans—in the latter half of the 20th century are so accustomed to deciphering and understanding photographs, that it is easy to forget how we have learned the process and how good we have become at it. Beginning in the last half of the 19th century, and as a result of more and more unretouched photographs being reproduced in magazines, newspapers and books (first pioneered by *Life* magazine in the 1930s), the collective eye has learned to obtain information from photographs.

More and more historians realize that there can be much information gathered from photographs—signs in shop windows, the dress of the persons pictured, the date of the carriage or car parked at the curb, and thousands of other details that help them understand a time and place.

In a prescient set of his essays *(Half a Truth is Better Than None,* University of Chicago Press, 1982), John A. Kouwenhoven notes a significant change in our conception of history due to the advent of the snapshot in "Living in a Snapshot World" and "Photographs as Historical Documents." Kouwenhoven writes that, "history for many centuries was ... something untrustworthily reported that happened long ago. Thanks—or no thanks—to the snapshot, history is now what we live in from the moment we are old enough to look at pictures. That is one consequence of the modern technology of visual communication. Our 'now' instantaneously becomes history, and for most of us 'history' is our own immediate present."

It is recognized that the snapshot has changed how we view our world today. Snapshots show us the world in a way that is different from the manner in which our unaided eyes see. Kouwenhoven writes that we all "live, without realizing it, in a world of which we are aware primarily because of photography." Yet, while a snapshot is "a window on the past [it is] ... only a fossilized unstoried instant whose significance may be undiscoverable unless other data, visual or verbal, is available." Kouwenhoven notes that photographs are historical documents, but that they are "nonnarrative" and "nonfictitious."

Unlike a painting or a word picture (both of which can contain details from various times, gathered together by the artist or the writer) Kouwenhoven wisely suggests, "the camera lens is ... indiscriminate," for "a photographic negative is determined by the impartial objectivity of light," and "whatever hierarchy of forms appears in the snapshot is ordained by the indiscriminate neutrality of light."

As selective as a historian, who gathers what might be considered the more important facts for a treatise on a particular subject, the photographer and the photograph editor must use their experienced judgment to bring information to the viewer. The photographs in *One Average Day* have gone through that careful, selective process. Historians will look back on this book as an effort, done with intelligence and insight, to record our times.

The directors of Project Dayshoot were careful in their planning and preparation for the day's shooting. Meetings, discussions, differences of opinion led to the many photographic assignments—and the added provision for each photographer to keep an eye open for anything special. The directors and the many participating photographers did a magnificent job; all should be congratulated and pleased with the results. These photographs are but a fraction of the thousands of images recorded on 15 July 1983, and only a small portion of the several thousand submitted for consideration by the more than ninety professional photographers involved.

It has been said that a photograph does not lie, but that photographers can distort, through the manipulation of the image. The professionals who took these images are practiced at making quick decisions that are accurate. These photographs do not lie. These are honest photographs. Most of them were taken by experienced photojournalists, persons who must take direct and straightforward pictures daily. On the whole, the selection made by the photograph editors, and reproduced here in *One Average Day,* is positive, human and kind, attributes that seem to represent the state of Oregon.

By definition, much was missed. That could not be avoided. However, the planning that took place prior to the date of shooting enabled a phenomenal amount of visual material to be recorded. That planning was absolutely necessary.

However, when *the* day arrived, time began to fly—there was the quiet "well, here it is," among all the participants. The sense of slipping time, of not enough time, was balanced by all the homework, all the care and all the professional acumen that the directors and the professional photographers could provide. It was an impressive organizational and committed effort.

This collection of Oregon photographs records events, persons and places from almost every county in the state, from every level of life (economic, social and philosophical), picturing the broad mosaic that is Oregon. These photographs show persons hard at work and unemployed. They record the beginning of life and the nearness of death. They find humor and desperation. They show Oregonians as either day or night people, urban or rural dwellers. They look at the state from inside buildings, along roadways, in field and forest, at play and toiling, from the air and on the water. All four borders of the state are here (as well as Oregon's geographic center), and every hour of the day.

The illustrations offer the arts and commerce. There are politicians caught in the consternations of modern problems, police and fire fighters, new religions and old, contemporary skylines and abandoned dwellings. Video games and card playing, physical therapy, aerobics and world-class athletes are here, as are shipping, railroading, trucks and tired feet. There are idle hands and hands calloused by hard work.

There is good food and the "worst food." There are old ways and new trends, animals and machines. Some persons stand openly naked, some fear the camera's intrusion.

Abroad, on the day photographers were recording thousands of images for *One Average Day,* events were transpiring that drew the attention of Oregonians reading and watching the news.

The difficulty of the struggle of Solidarity and the church against the repressive regime in Poland was again highlighted with the day's announcement that the Polish leaders would continue many of the more restrictive features of the current martial law in that country. Some lessening of East-West tension seemed forthcoming, as the United States and the Soviet Union reached a major agreement at a conference in Madrid on the 1975 Helsinki human rights accords.

On 15 July one of the many terrorist groups that plague our times again struck, when the Armenian Secret Army for the Liberation of Armenia bombed the Turkish Airlines' ticket counter at Orly Airport in Paris—five were killed, and many others injured. Troubles continued in Lebanon, Northern Ireland (where youths attacked police in Londonderry) and in Central America (where the government of Nicaragua claimed that Honduras-based rebels were about to attack).

In the first known reversal of a death sentence in Japan, a man was released from prison after spending 12,598 days behind bars. On an equally happy note, and one that always gives a hint of promise and hope for the world's future, 15,000 scouts from 101 countries were breaking camp at the 15th World Scout Jamboree in Calgary, Alberta.

Nationally, it was disclosed on this Friday that during the 1980 presidential campaign the Reagan organization obtained material from the Carter camp, which enabled former California governor Reagan to better prepare for nationally televised debates with incumbent President Jimmy Carter. And, in New Orleans, Vice President George Bush defended the Reagan Administration's policies at the annual convention of the NAACP. In Washington, D.C., on 15 July, moves were made to block funding for the MX nuclear missile.

Stocks dropped sharply on Friday—ending a losing week at the two major stock exchanges. However, the American dollar was at its highest level in seven years against the increasingly weak West German D-Mark.

Heat records were set in many parts of the country; New York City recorded an all-time high for the day, reaching a humid 99 degrees. As a result of this heat wave, and as a comment on the cooler-than-normal

Oregon temperatures, Bend's newspaper, the *Bulletin,* had as its lead headline, "Northwest shivers as nation swelters." Parts of Texas were suffering nine inches of rain, while further north and west the absence of precipitation was providing conditions for brush fires in Nevada, California, Utah, Montana and Oregon.

Nationally, the high temperature for the day was recorded—as it often is—at Gila Bend, Arizona, where it was over 116 degrees. The lowest high temperature was to be found at Butte, Montana, where it only reached 34. Around the state of Oregon, no spot recorded a low temperature that could match Butte's high; Baker, one of the lowest, dropped to 37 on the morning of the 15th. Brookings, on the southwest coast, recorded the state's high with 76 degrees, but both Lakeview, in the southeast, and Salem, in the central Willamette Valley, were in the 70s. Portland reached no higher than 68 during the day.

In Oregon there was some rain: some, because it was July; rain, because it is Oregon. Overcast skies covered much of the state. There were traces of rain in some sections. Seaside had .11 of an inch and Portland .01. However, this light rain belied the above-average count for both July (.98 inches above normal) and for the year to date (7.35 inches above the normal 19.80 inches).

Sunrise on the 15th was 5:36 AM and the sun set at 8:57 PM.

National events affecting Oregon directly were many. President Reagan announced that he would preside at a meeting of the Cabinet Council on Natural Resources and the Environment in a gathering that would discuss federal timber contract relief in the Pacific Northwest. In another forestry-related action, federal and state officials agreed to attempt a compromise plan for reserving "old growth" timber in the Coos Bay District of the Bureau of Land Management.

Oregon U.S. Senator Mark Hatfield announced on the Dayshoot Friday that more than one hundred million dollars for water-related projects in Oregon had been allocated by the federal government.

Part of an ongoing debate among a number of concerned parties led federal and Oregon state officials to postpone a decision to close commercial salmon fishing along a portion of the Oregon coast. However, it was agreed to extend the fishing season for Columbia River treaty Indians along that river.

Around the state there were many occurrences that made *One Average Day,* 15 July 1983, unique.

The Oregon House of Representatives adjourned its regular session at 11:10 PM. Exactly 79 minutes later, in the early morning hours of 16 July, the State Senate would follow suit. The 62nd Legislative Assembly was officially closed without solving the knotty problem of tax relief and whither a sales tax. Governor Victor Atiyeh promised to have members of both houses back in special session soon.

As usual, all manner of local government and concerns were manifested throughout the state, exemplified by the meeting at 7:30 PM of the Gresham Sign Review Committee at a local pancake house.

On Friday, 15 July 1983 five Oregon cities—Bend, Hillsboro, Klamath Falls, La Grande and The Dalles—were named winners of the state-wide Oregon Main Street Competition—a private sector move to revitalize the cores of Oregon's cities.

Among the many environmental questions facing Oregonians, none was more prominent than the ongoing controversy about the preservation of the Columbia Gorge.

In Salem, a two-quart spill of PCB from a PGE power pole capacitator, which it was feared endangered a pregnant woman living nearby, was deemed safe by a representative of the power company.

At noon, in downtown Portland's Schrunk Plaza, there was an official 'kickoff' celebration by participants in the 1983 Scottish Highland Games (the event taking place at David Douglas High School).

Elsewhere in the City of Roses, some northeast Portland apartment dwellers were forced to vacate their building because it was feared that the structure was in danger from adjacent excavation along the Banfield light-rail construction area. Another transportation-related issue was faced, with the announcement of a tentative new location for a riverside heliport in Portland.

In his day-long visit to Oregon's largest city, former Black Panther leader Eldridge Cleaver spoke of his conversion to Christianity. And at that city's Civic Stadium, Jamie Reynolds and Shery Otos were married at home plate prior to the Portland Beaver's PCL game against the Tacoma Tigers (the Beavers won the game by a score of seven to six to remain at the top of the league).

At the Portland City Club, Jeffrey Whitehorn, a New York investment analyst, chastised Northwesterners for allowing the nationally known WPPSS (Washington Public Power Supply System) fiasco to take place. At the same time, at a luncheon of the Bend Chamber of Commerce, a Portland advertising executive suggested that Oregon tourism offices be established in both Germany and Japan.

Two older buildings in downtown Medford collapsed for no apparent reason at 9:20 in the evening; no one was injured. On that morning, one thousand customers were without electricity in the Beaverton area after a truck hit a power pole. In the coastal community of Lincoln City, members of the police department voted to approve a new one-year contract. A man was killed in Roseburg when the forklift he was driving overturned and trapped him. Two Portland men were treated for gunshot wounds after they had had an argument.

Eight freighters arrived in the Portland area or at various ports along the Columbia River. An equal number of ships laden with goods from Oregon left on the 15th to travel the Pacific.

There were many cultural events and activities taking place around the state. Carol Channing was appearing at Portland's Civic Auditorium in the classic Broadway musical, *Hello Dolly!* Yelling at the crowd at that city's popular music mecca, Starry Night, Barry Melton of the Dinosaurs said: "I know what you're thinkin', that we're a bunch of burned out hippies!" (The group is composed of former players from 1960's San Francisco rock bands.) The Moon Country Sno-Mobilers were having a benefit rummage sale at Bend Plaza.

At the Oregon Historical Society an interesting exhibit, "The Artists Patecky," was highlighting decades of contributions by three members of a talented Portland-area family. Across Park Avenue from the Historical Center, at the Art Museum, the popular "Frozen Image—Scandinavian Photography" show was in place. In the Berg Swann Auditorium the annual Mystery Writers' Convention was being held—authors Amanda Cross, Joseph Hansen and Tony Hillerman were present.

In the state capital, the 10-day, 36th annual National Appaloosa Horse Show was nearing the end of its run at the Oregon State Fairgrounds. Elsewhere in Salem, that city's art festival, called this year, "Rainbows of Color," opened for its 34th annual run. Cottage Grove was celebrating Bohemia Mining Days, and in Jefferson that community's Mint Festival was in progress. Chamber Music Northwest was presenting a concert at the Columbia Gorge Hotel near Hood River, renowned Oregon poet William Stafford was reading his works at Oregon State University, and "Star Gazing at Timberline" was drawing evening viewers at the new Wy'East Daylodge. At Breitenbush in the central Cascades the "Rolling Thunder Workshop" was in full swing during the day, and there was an evening presentation entitled "Champoeg," at its namesake state park.

Of course, Oregon's most famous theatrical location was filled with eager enthusiasts of the Bard, as the Oregon Shakespearean Festival continued its long summer run in Ashland, presenting *Cymbeline* and George Bernard Shaw's *Man and Superman*. On a smaller scale, a Portland State University group was presenting a play at Cannon Beach's Coaster Theatre.

The movies showing at first-run theaters were, among others, *War Games, Return of the Jedi, Staying Alive, Trading Places, Superman III, Porky's II, Twilight Zone, Stroker Ace, Fanny and Alexander;* on this "one average day," the Disney movie *Snow White* was re-released.

On evening television, part four of the ABC dramatization of "Masada" was running against the CBS favorite "Dallas." On PBS, "A Town like Alice" was in its second installment. The "Dukes of Hazzard" and "Benson" drew their regular television viewing audiences around the state.

In sports, besides the Portland Beaver win, the two major leagues were drawing the attention of baseball fans. Lee Trevino finished his round to lead the British Open, and the Pacific Northwest Golf Association Tournament was drawing local interest at the Tualatin Golf Club. The Oregon State Tennis Championships were taking place at Portland's eastside Irvington Club. Further to the east in the metropolitan area, the summer dog racing program continued at the Multnomah Kennel Club at Fairview.

At one of Eugene's popular all-comers meets at the University of Oregon's Hayward Field, Jim Hill defeated local favorites Alberto Salazar and Ron Tabb in a relatively slow 10,000 meters—recording a time of 27 minutes and 59.5 seconds. There were 4,500 spectators at this Friday evening meet, and they also cheered wins by three different members of the McChesney family of Eugene.

This listing of events and occasions is but a fractional indication of the many others taking place during the 24-hours that were covered in Project Dayshoot.

It was *One Average Day*. It was summer, it was 15 July, and it was 1983. The photographs that follow chronicle Oregon and Oregonians in a magnificent fashion, the result of the composite talent of many talented persons. The photographs from 15 July 1983 are a panorama, a panoply and a visual record of *One Average Day*.

Bruce Taylor Hamilton

ONE AVERAGE DAY

ALVORD DESERT / 10:45 PM to 4:15 AM /
KEITH SKELTON

BOARDMAN / 5:30 AM / STEVE NEHL

This time-lapse view of star trails (below) appropriately introduces the nearly three hundred photographs in this book. Keith Skelton records the movement of the Oregon landscape under the night sky as 14 July turned into "One Average Day," 15 July 1983. The photographer camped out in this area near Steens Mountain.

Day breaks on the imposing coal-fired power plant at Boardman (opposite page). The stack is one of the tallest structures in the state.

2

ONE AVERAGE DAY

1
BEFORE DAWN

Beginning their work against the dying night, the several Oregon photographers represented here in this opening chapter stole out into the lingering darkness where the soul of Oregon can be captured unaware. Dawn: a kind of bargain time between soft sleep and the first realities of the morning—how sweet the air can be!

Morning is both dark and light—it is "reveille" for some and "taps" for others. It can be a time of anticipation or a bleaker time of gritty-eyed coffee drinking, when life's emotional hangovers are either anticipated or endured.

For some, the morning begins alone—waking, one might listen to the simple miracle of one's own heart, beating. For others, the morning begins together, wrapped in each other's arms, and sharing warmth, sharing love. For some, it is a time to have babies or to feed them. For others, it is a time to sit and stare, watch over friends, or to wait and watch for life's slow ships to come in. It is a time when freight trains push ghosts before them in the humid farm-field air, when leviathan trucks huddle like gossipy aluminum matrons.

In 1936 H. L. Davis won the Pulitzer Prize for his novel, *Honey In The Horn*. It is a classic and perhaps the greatest novel about Oregon. Davis, a journalist and poet, wrote about his state in the early 1900s. His mind was a camera and he developed literary snapshots with his imagination that touched his readers and awakened their emotions.

That is what these photographers want you to do—to feel. They want to attract your attention, they want to let you roam with them. They want to show you what it is to awake on an Oregon morning, and move through the day; through the work, the worry, the laughter and human vagaries of life represented in this book, showing people in homes, at work, in fields beneath a broad summer's sky.

Each photographer has probed his or her heart for appropriate symbols to represent this most personal time of day. Keith Skelton opens the shutter of his camera out on the Oregon desert, and spends a sleepless night watching (as does his camera) the night turn into day.

In northwest Portland, across the state from Skelton, Marv Bondarowicz records the urban night lights. Because so many persons are asleep at this time, no other sector of *One Average Day* has such a high proportion of persons at work, working in cafes, gas and police stations, rail yards, hospitals and as a mother at home.

Each one of us, including the photographers who have caught these precious hours of a day's first light, cannot know what a day will hold. Yet the promise of the morning is the promise of hope, as most of us wake and take up our daily lives.

1. PORTLAND / 12:00 AM / MARV
   BONDAROWICZ

2. PORTLAND / 12:37 AM / MARV
   BONDAROWICZ

1. Sometimes a new day comes too early to sort all at once. It must be eased into, and coffee is required — lots of it. Fryer's Quality Pie, or "Q.P.," is a Portland institution. Northwest Portlanders know the Q.P. as a place of thoughts and reflections, where it is never quite night or day. So, it is a good place to start.

2. Harry Rogers is a nightly regular at the Q.P., sitting for a long spell solving *Oregonian* crossword puzzles.

1

2

3. PORTLAND / 12:02 AM / MARV
BONDAROWICZ

4. PORTLAND / 12:07 AM / MARV
BONDAROWICZ

3. A former Portlander now living in California, Dr. Thomas Farnham is visiting his northwest Portland family. Whenever he visits, he always makes a trip to the Q.P.

4. Finished with their pies and cups of coffee, Greg Sage (left) and Brad Davidson sit and survey the "scene" at the Q.P.

4

3

5. Police dispatcher Irene Lutz has finished her shift at this Coos County town of Powers and waits for a ride home with officer Gary Ellis.

5

6. The sound of silence is never as loud as it is in a sleeping hospital ward when the night holds its breath and takes a count before dawn. It is never as dark as it is then, either. Kris Edwards, a registered nurse, maintains her vigil at the monitors in the Intensive Care Unit of Hillsboro's Tuality Community Hospital.

7. Weather display screen at Portland International Airport offers a taste of 15 July's hazy skies to incoming travelers collecting their baggage.

6

7

LATEST HOURLY OBSERVATIONS

LOCATION	°F	RH	SKY/WX	WIND
PORTLAND	57	76	P CLDY	CALM
EUGENE	51	82	P CLDY	CALM
SALEM	56	71	P CLDY	W 4
MEDFORD	57	63	CLEAR	W 5
NORTH BEND	57	79	P CLDY	N 8
NEWPORT	59	76	CLOUDY	N 5
ASTORIA	57	85	M CLDY	W 7

FRI JUL 15   1:05:51 AM

LOCAL TEMPERATURE   56°F

8. COBURG / 2:15 AM / BETTY UDESEN

9. COBURG / 2:30 AM / BETTY UDESEN

8. Truck 'n Travel, a truckstop at the Coburg exit along I-5, where rigs are parked in a line. In them their weary drivers catch some sleep before they move on toward their destinations.

9. Ralph Blum's fueling up before heading north to Seattle. Ralph, 37, has driven a truck for seven years — one with his own rig. He carries roofing supplies and says, "It's hard to make ends meet." Having just driven out of southern California, Ralph finds the Oregon morning chilly.

8

9

8

10. SPRINGFIELD / 4:45 AM / BETTY UDESEN

11. SPRINGFIELD / 4:45 AM / BETTY UDESEN

10. John Becker stands at the doorway of his Springfield freight office. Becker has been working for railroads for 45 years. "Of course now, we don't get as much business as we did before the recession," he said, although between 50 and 60 trains pass by the station during his 12:00 to 8:00 AM shift.

11. Startled by a photographer who noticed his light, Southern Pacific train clerk John Becker records information on a freight car in the Springfield yard.

11

10

12. It is quarter to three and there is no one in the place but photographer Charlie Nye, his wife, Lori (calling friends to tell them that her labor had begun), his one-year-old son, Jeremy, and an insistent, yet-to-be-born baby. With his Nikon, Charlie will introduce us to his daughter, Abby Ruth, at 5:56 AM in photograph 20.

13. Some might call it getting a clean start in the petroleum industry. Attendant Ray Lauer, 22, of Tigard, might just call it lonely, as he cleans a Standard station on Portland's Barbur Boulevard.

14. The aroma of pecan rolls hot out of the oven drew the photographer through the propped-open front door. Busy through the night, bakers Peter Dallman (left) and John Denning are almost midway through their shift at northwest Portland's "Chocolate Raspberry," finishing 72 Kaiser rolls and 12 rolls of Challah for the Sabbath.

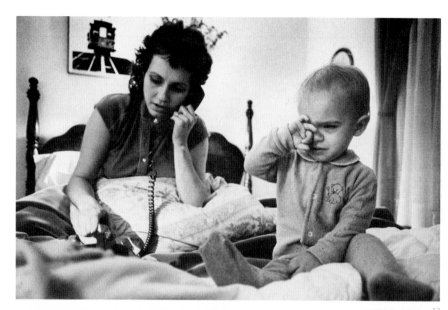

12

13

14

15. Each half asleep, a mother and child
share the need that will bond them for a
lifetime. Photographer Dana Olsen cap-
tures a Madonna-like portrait of his wife,
Constance, and his 14-week-old daughter,
Anika Marie, at their northwest Portland
home.

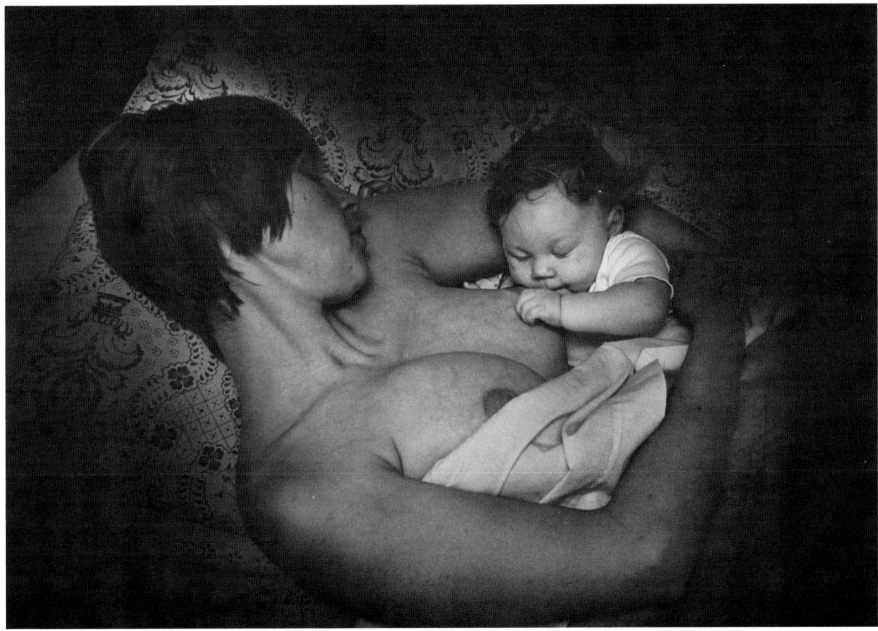

15

COLUMBIA RIVER / 6:40 AM / ED VIDINGHOFF
PORTLAND / 8:16 AM / ROSS HAMILTON
EUGENE / 8:00 AM / DAN BATES
BURNS / 6:00 AM / GREGORY J. LAWLER
NEAR ASHLAND / 8:40 AM / CHRISTOPHER BRISCOE
COLUMBIA GORGE / 8:50 AM / MICHAEL PARKER

Early morning mist and fog shroud the Trojan Nuclear Power Plant on the Oregon side of the Columbia River near Rainier (top left). The ship is about to head down river toward the mouth of the Columbia at Astoria, leaving Kalama, Washington.

It is morning, beginning another long day in Portland's skid road area (center left).

One of the many transients (center) living near West 1st Street in Eugene, near the Eugene Mission. This fellow refers to himself as "The King."

An ultralight (flown by Brian Lansburgh) and a hot-air balloon (under the controls of balloonist Nancy Lochrie) are frozen in midflight (lower center) by photographer Christopher Briscoe from his perch in a 1941 Stearman biplane (piloted by George DiMartini).

The old Sod House School in Burns barely stands above the high waters that plagued southeastern Oregon during this spring and summer.

Aerial photographer Michael Parker, piloting his own plane, focuses on the Columbia Gorge west of Hood River (opposite page). His altitude here is eight hundred feet.

12

ONE AVERAGE DAY

2
MORNING

If you are elderly, you might be working on memories. If you have had a long life, you might speak of old photographs, especially in summer, if there is no rain and if someone asks you about your life.

Often, in the early morning, children are born; if they are a bit older than newborn, they might be asking where parents go, and what is it that they do? If they are out on an average day, they might just be capturing the wonderful experience of morning; asking about birds, or watching clouds like those in El Greco skies, hoping for the warm weather that makes young days seem to last forever.

There are images from around the state, from all four borders and the geographical center of Oregon at Post; from Portland, Salem and Eugene-Springfield; from Lafayette, Hillsboro, McMinnville and Astoria; from over the Columbia and the Pacific Ocean, near Ukiah, Echo, Oakridge and Hells Canyon.

Between young and old is the majority of this state's workers. For many working people the hours before ten in the morning have a cheerful, optimistic quality. Muscles loosen in the warmth of exertion, if you are physically employed. If not, your fingers find the keys and the mind calls for the appropriate productivity. It is a fine time on a summer morning, those hours before noon, before lunch, when you know at day's halftime how that day, already in motion, will probably conclude.

But what if these morning hours are filled only with a dreadful ennui? What if there was no work, only the grimy disappointment of unemployment? What if you were under Portland's bridges and living there? Are these persons perhaps hoping things will improve?

What do you say when someone asks you what you do? Everybody does something. Whether it is praying or waiting, living or dying or just moving around, looking for hope; looking and finding and knowing about life.

There are three views of the mighty Columbia River here (two in color); Michael Parker was in the air and Ed Vidinghoff sees Oregon across the river from the Washington side.

There are many at work. This is the time in an average day when so much labor begins. But, there are many who seem to have no hope for employment.

There is the juxtaposition of a naked man in a sweatlodge and a heavily clothed Coast Guardsman. Robert Pennell shows us groggy ranch hands, Dan Bates and Ross Hamilton portray those sadly out of work.

There are proud faces here. There is industriousness, foolishness and therapy. There are faces full of young hope, belief and future; there are faces that seem to look back over long, good lives.

This chapter explodes with life. A score of photographers went out and found it between 4:00 and 10:00 AM. 'What is it that you do?' they ask. Here are some of the answers.

16. It is 4:00 AM in the Hawkins farm
bunkhouse, and Wray Hawkins, Jr., (left)
and his brother Kelly contemplate another
day of driving back-and-forth on the family fields, putting in another 16 hours, getting in the wheat harvest.

16

ONE AVERAGE DAY

17. NEAR ECHO / 6:00 AM / ROBERT PENNELL

18. LAFAYETTE / 5:05 AM / TOM BALLARD

19. HILLSBORO / 5:35 AM / MICHAL THOMPSON

17. Early morning has its established symbols, one of them being a cup of coffee. Here Emmett Steiner, who cooks for the Hawkins farm, pours some java for the wheat harvest hands. In trade for his help, the Hawkins family harvests wheat on Steiner's small farm nearby.

18. His face and hands uplifted in prayer, Father Timothy Michelle, a Trappist monk, celebrates a 5:00 AM Mass at the Abbey of Our Lady of Guadalupe near Lafayette.

19. Brian Gould sets up Hillsboro (here, at a stand in front of McDonalds) for the world's daily announcements on his early morning *USA Today* paper route.

17

19

18

20. SPRINGFIELD / 5:56 AM / CHARLIE NYE

21. PORTLAND / 7:15 AM / BARBARA F. GUNDLE

20. As new as the day into which she is born, little Abby Ruth Nye (only a labor pain in photograph 12) comes into the world to the wonder of her parents. Charlie Nye, who was by his wife's side during her labor, took the photograph at the moment of birth with a bulb extension release. This midwife-assisted birth took place at Springfield's McKenzie-Willamette Hospital.

21. While little Abby Ruth was introduced to her first and rather chaotic morning, Rebecca Wyan Lawler Gundle, otherwise—and perhaps more conveniently — known as "Munchie," says goodbye to her photographer mother from the front porch of her northeast Portland home.

21

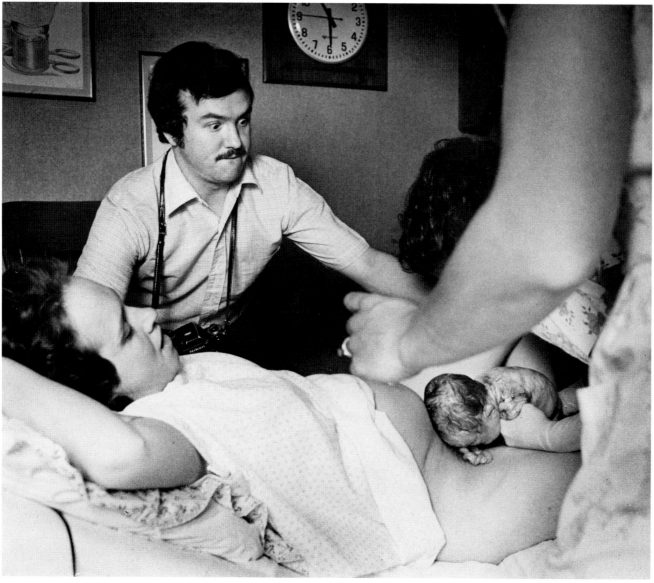

20

22. SPRINGFIELD / 5:56 AM / CHARLIE NYE

22. "It's a boy!" "No! It's a girl!" It was Abby Ruth Nye's umbilical cord that caused her mother's initial confusion, quickly straightened out by midwife Penny Harmon immediately following the baby's delivery. But the words that came first from mother Lori Borgman-Nye were, "Thank you, God."

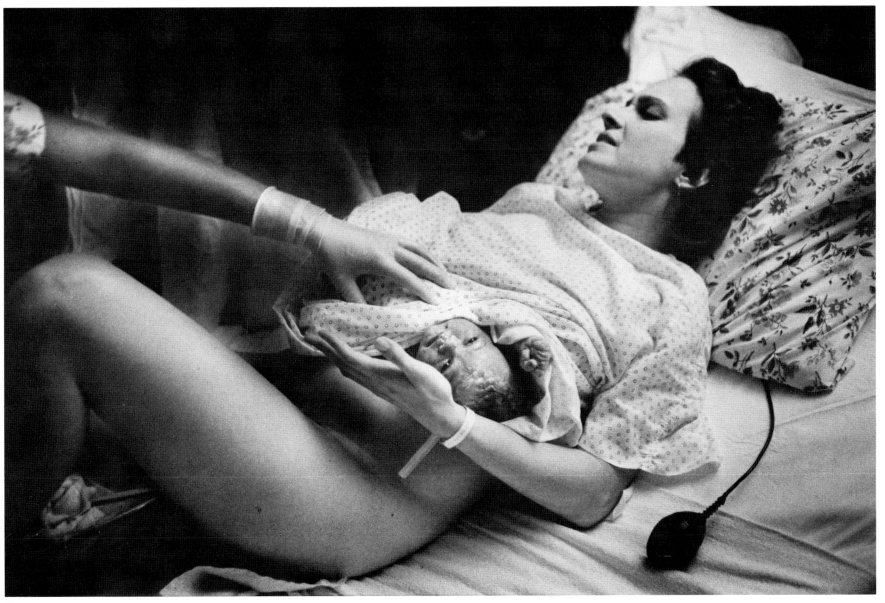

22

23. Robert Adams, avionicsman second class, wears a helmet, flight suit, goggles, gloves and microphone, all necessary for his work surveying the Pacific coastline. Here, 30 miles off the Washington coast, Adams sits in a chair positioned at the doorway of the Astoria-based Coast Guard Law Enforcement Patrol helicopter, a position from which he can better aid injured or endangered persons.

24. About to head for a day's work in the forests outside Springfield, a Weyer-haeuser crew sits in a company bus. There is some time for contemplating the work ahead, and it is the time to change from street shoes to work boots.

23

24

25. SALEM / 7:45 AM / MICHAEL LLOYD

26. UMATILLA INDIAN RESERVATION / 7:00 AM / JOEL DAVIS

25. Standing in his office in the State Capitol, on what would be the long-awaited closing day of the session of the Oregon Legislature, House Speaker Grattan Kerans (awaiting a meeting with Senate President Ed Fadeley to discuss legislative strategy on property tax relief) takes a quick scan of the *Oregonian*.

26. In an Indian sweathouse near McKay Creek, about 15 miles east of Pendleton, Ron Pond splashes water on heated rocks in a manner traditional to Indians for centuries. The door of the sweathouse, by tradition, faces east to greet the sun.

26

25

27. OREGON-NEVADA BORDER /
8:00 AM / DAVE SWAN

28. COLUMBIA RIVER GORGE /
8:50 AM / MICHAEL PARKER

29. OREGON-NEVADA BORDER /
6:00 AM / DAVE SWAN

27. The southeast corner. The sun shines brightly over the John Nouque Ranch, a family operation since the turn of the century; the ranch occupies 640 acres in three states (Oregon, Idaho and Nevada). The heavy rains of 1983 filled nearby ditches to overflowing and created head-high grasses. This photograph was taken on the Oregon side of the border near McDermitt, Nevada.

28. The northern border. Almost directly over the watery demarcation between Oregon and Washington, and flying just 800 feet above the Columbia River between Cascade Locks and Hood River, aerial photographer Michael Parker takes this westward view.

29. The southern border. Two transients coming from McDermitt, Nevada, cross into Oregon.

27

28

29

30. NEAR IMNAHA / 7:00 AM / DAVID WEINTRAUB

31. POST / 7:30 AM / LYLE COX

32. CHARLESTON / 7:30 AM / BRUCE W. SMITH

30. The eastern border. The first light of 15 July 1983 touches Oregon. This view is to the west from the Five Mile Observation Site in the Hells Canyon Recreation Area, near the Imnaha River. Tony Metcalf is about to survey this remarkable vista through his binoculars.

31. The center of Oregon. The general store and Elkhorn Tavern at Post. Seen as a blur—and the only vehicle to pass this spot for 45 minutes, a Forest Service truck moves through what may be Oregon's true "central business district." Post lies almost exactly in the center of the state.

32. The western border. This serene view of Charleston harbor (which lies on South Slough just west of the city of Coos Bay) belies the turmoil surrounding these fishing boats. Instead of being in the rolling waters of the Pacific, on this day the fishermen who own these boats were in Salem protesting the low salmon prices and the small size of the fish being taken.

32

30

31

33.   In front of a house on Union's main street, a horse grazes on a well-kept lawn.

33

34. BETWEEN NYE AND UKIAH /
     7:00 AM / RICH IWASAKI

34.   This photograph was taken from U.S.
Highway 395, about 35 miles southwest of
Pendleton and not far from Battle Mountain State Park. This horse grazes in more
normal circumstances than the one pictured on the facing page.

34

35. NEAR OAKRIDGE / 6:00 AM / VANESSA MCVAY

36. NEAR OAKRIDGE / 8:00 AM / VANESSA MCVAY

37. NEAR SPRINGFIELD / 8:30 AM / BETTY UDESEN

35. After cutting a wedge from a 400-foot Douglas fir, logger Dave McMurrick pauses for a moment to make a last-minute check of the tree's top. Working on part of Pope and Talbot's thirty thousand acres in this area south of Oakridge, McMurrick and other timber men are felling "oldgrowth."

36. Near Oakridge, a hillside in the Rigdon District of Willamette National Forest is mute testimony to modern clear-cut methods of logging.

37. A modern loader lifts a log at a Weyerhaeuser logging site off Deer Creek Road. This log will be transported to the company's operation in Springfield.

35

36

37

38. EUGENE / 6:00 AM / DAN BATES

39. NEAR LAPINE / 6:30 AM / DALE SWANSON

38. Mike Evans, 13, does his part, gleaning small change (for himself, his mother and sister) from the returnable cans and bottles left by lovers' lane litterbugs on Eugene's Skinner Butte. Part of the Emerald City's growing civic pride, the newly completed Hult Center and Hilton Hotel can be seen in the foreground; Spencer Butte lies in the distance.

39. Meanwhile—and taken at almost the same time as Dan Bate's Eugene photograph — Dale Swanson records this view near LaPine, at a popular wooded roadside location where "campers" often stop overnight. Despite the posted admonition, unsightly debris litters the ground.

39

38

40. ASTORIA / 10:00 AM / BILL WAGNER

41. MT. ANGEL / 8:30 AM / CATHY CHENEY

42. PORTLAND / 9:00 AM / BARBARA F. GUNDLE

40. In touch with the past, Astoria's Vera Gault has transformed her upstairs hallway into a photographic museum of her family. She has been involved with many historical preservation activities in the city, one of which is a guide she prepared for walking tours of Astoria's fine old homes.

41. "Good morning." Sister Teresa, nurse at the Benedictine Sisters Nursing Home in Mt. Angel, greets a patient with a tender touch during her morning rounds.

42. Snuggled with her mother, Feriha Kunt, in their Portland home, Sevin Hirschbein returns the love she received as a child. Her mother suffers from Alzheimer's Disease and is no longer able to speak.

40

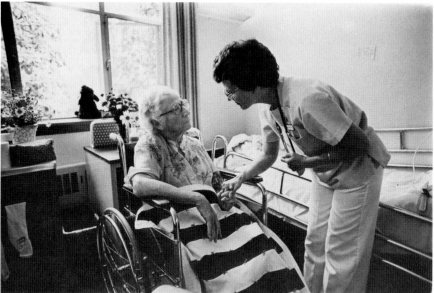

41

42

43. PORTLAND / 7:30 AM / BARBARA F. GUNDLE

44. MCMINNVILLE / 9:55 AM / TOM BALLARD

43. In the cab of her water truck, which is used to wet down sand on I-84 construction site near Portland's NE 33rd Avenue, Teamster I.V. Heiman represents the expanded job opportunities available to women today.

44. Keying in data on a Oregon Mutual Insurance Co. computer is Nancy Holmes (foreground), flanked by her colleagues (left to right) Sandy Hoffstadt, Cindy Murphy and Angela McGanty. These four women work at a firm founded here in McMinnville in 1894, one of the first mutual insurance companies west of the Mississippi.

44

43

45. PORTLAND / 7:15 AM / ROSS
     HAMILTON

46. PORTLAND / 6:40 AM / ROSS
     HAMILTON

45. It can be a gray, mean cityscape on skid road; meaner and grayer beneath a hard, unpromising summer sky. This photograph was taken at the corner of Burnside and NW Second Avenue in Portland.

46. Not far away, and half-an-hour earlier, Hamilton records this scene of desolation in Portland's skid road. As soon as the photograph was taken, the man got up and walked away. (Photographer Ross Hamilton, who started the day on Portland's skid road, would have photography visits in the mayor's office and with an evening baseball game, and would eventually finish shooting at a popular Portland-area music spot at the very end of the day.)

45

46

47. PORTLAND / 7:35 AM / ROSS
     HAMILTON

48. PORTLAND / 6:20 AM / ROSS
     HAMILTON

47. Standing outside Portland's "Old Town" Salvation Army building, a man named "Ted" stands stern faced and wearing an "I Love Skid Row Road" button.

48. This trio, "Boxcar Mary," "Spike" and "Pop" calm themselves by a fire under a Portland freeway ramp on the east bank of the Willamette River. They are contemplating moving on to a new town; just three hours earlier they had been attacked by some men who tried to take their food, clothing and cooking gear. Spike said it was an "omen" for them to move on.

48

47

49. EUGENE / 8:45 AM / DAN BATES

50. NEAR SPRINGFIELD / 9:00 AM / BETTY UDESEN

51. NEAR ECHO / 6:00 AM / ROBERT PENNELL

52. UNION / 9:42 AM / RON COOPER

49. David "Cage" Campbell, 33, has been unemployed for eight years, since leaving the Merchant Marine. He is here photographed near the Eugene Mission on 1st Street.

50. Ray Haase is a shop mechanic for Weyerhaeuser — or "Weyco" as he calls it. He has been with the forest products company since 1965.

51. Guild Lay. Born in 1906 at Hibley, Lay ran a cattle ranch at Medical Springs. "I loved ranching [there] … but we were always fighting the snow or forest fires…. Things got too tough and we moved down here."

52. Bob Hawkins, on the Hawkins farm near Echo, directs the operation of seven combines and a half-dozen trucks; all used to harvest wheat and haul it to local grain elevators.

49

52

50

51

53. HILLSBORO / 9:15 AM / MICHAL
THOMPSON

53. At Hillsboro's 11-acre Camp Ireland,
which serves 1,200 boys each summer (one
of the nation's largest day camps) Cub
Scouts hold their week-long Sunset Trail
Day Camp. Celebrating the final day of
camp, Webelo Eric Nilson participates in
the morning flag-raising ceremony. Perhaps anticipating the rite of passage to
becoming a Boy Scout he salutes with three
fingers instead of two.

53

54. HILLSBORO / 9:40 AM / MICHAL THOMPSON

54. Donna Ogden instructs her class (left to right: Hazel Sounenir, Norine Teachout, J. "Ted" Jensen, Ogden and Regina Miner) in a session of water therapy and exercise for senior citizens at the two-year-old Hillsboro Aquatic Center.

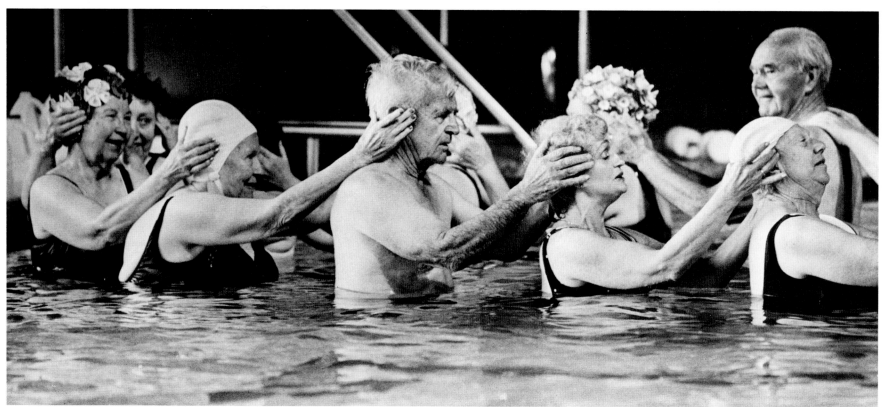

54

55.   Proving what their wives told them all along, these "Jackasses," new members of The Order of the Antelope, participate in a bizarre, beer can-rolling initiation rite that crosses the line between Deschutes and Lake counties.

56.   On a busier roadway between Imnaha and Joseph, more sensible beasts move much more gracefully. Cars and cows share the road, but as the photographer wrote: "Sometimes the cows hog the highway. These cows aren't horsing around either. Cars sometimes play chicken with the cows, but cows are hard to outfox."

55

56

57. Kurt and his companion, "Little Bit," consider the future in their temporary Eugene home, a 1970 Dodge Charger. Out of work for some time, and staying near the "free soup at the Mission," the pair support themselves with money received for blood donations. Little Bit is pregnant. They do not know what they are going to do, but both love Oregon.

57

58.   Morning has much to do with yawning, stretching, planning or just washing windows. In his office in the State Capitol, Oregon House Speaker Grattan Kerans uses his arms expansively in a meeting with Senate President Ed Fadeley as the pair discuss the question of property tax relief and the possibility of a state sales tax.

59.   Steve Chambers' arms are utilized for more realistic tasks. He has been washing windows for four years — "It's fun, really!" Here he cleans the windows at Victoria's Nephew Restaurant in downtown Portland.

58

59

EUGENE / 2:00 PM / DAN BATES

NEAR HANCOCK FIELD STATION / 10:30 AM / KEVIN CLARK

NEAR WOODBURN / 1:16 PM / JILL A. CANNEFAX

EUGENE / 11:45 AM / DAN BATES

MT. HOOD / 11:25 AM / DAVID FALCONER

This laughing man (top left) is part of the colorful crowd of visitors at Eugene's 5th Street Public Market. Because of its many small shops and good food, the market is a favorite place to pass the time.

Wild sunflowers grow around an abandoned school house three miles east of Hancock Field Station in central Oregon (top center).

These five young girls — Natalia Boru, Kulina Ayhan, Marina Boru, Vassa Alazoz and Valia Alazoz (from left to right)—pose warily (top right) for photographer Jill Cannefax. They are part of a Russian community near Woodburn called the "Turkish Village," because most of the members came to America via Turkey.

This solitary laborer (bottom center) is painting parking meters next to Eugene's Oregon Electric Station.

A Crag Rat (bottom right)—a member of a Hood River-based climbing organization famous for its efforts at mountain rescue— sits on the porch outside Cloud Cap Inn, a nearly century-old lodge at timberline on Mt. Hood's northeast flank. Cloud Cap is used as base for mountain rescues, because many of the more dangerous climbing routes can be reached from this spot.

3
MIDDAY

Love, death and money are three basic themes which fascinate the average front-page newspaper reader. Fortunately for feature reporters and photojournalists, not all readers enjoy a steady diet of the basics and turn instead to the feature sections of a newspaper for a look at the human elements behind news events.

Unlike spot news photographs, a feature photograph demands more from a photojournalist or a freelancer than simply being in the right place at the right time. It demands a special twist of interest and skill which can transform the common appearance of a daily event into an eye-catching photograph that draws the reader into a story.

This chapter reveals many of the personal interests of the photographers. The photographers' admitted motivations range from interest in the everyday events of a small town, to the curiosity aroused by closed doors, to empathy with a struggle for survival.

Joel Davis's photograph of a continuous card game found in Pendleton's Club Cigar Restaurant is an example of a daily event which exists without any overtones of crucial news. The photograph documents both the card game and part of the atmosphere of an eastern Oregon town.

Michal Thompson's image of a 14-month-old child receiving his first haircut is another example of a universal, human picture many people might appreciate without the need to connect it with any news event.

Disclosing what is behind the closed doors of a protective community, a government agency, or finding the unexpected in a common subject is a challenge met by many of the Project Dayshoot participating photographers.

Beth Campbell discovered an eerie atmosphere at Bonneville Dam after walking away from the public areas. The dam is monitored by machines and workers are rarely seen.

Michael Lloyd's photograph of a discussion in the governor's office in Salem offers a rarely glimpsed moment of political diplomacy used by the governor when a potential stalemate is evident in the state legislature.

Not all of the photographers shooting during these hours accomplished what they set out to do. Sometimes years of experience, skill, and knowledge about a subject are simply not enough. For instance, after a morning of photographing transients, Don Bates attempted to photograph unemployed persons eating free meals at the Eugene Mission. "A tin filled with hot soup hit me square in the face, almost knocking me back a step," Bates wrote in the journal he kept for the day. "And before I could even wipe the gooey stuff out of my eyes [someone] said, 'You oughta ask somebody before taking my picture.'"

A photographer and reporter usually have more time during a feature assignment than a news assignment to establish a trusting relationship with the person or persons involved in a story. Bates was stopped before he even had a chance to start a discussion with the soup-line members.

Jill A. Cannefax almost struck out the first time she tried to photograph the Russian community in Woodburn because of the community members' distrust of cameras. Her first stop was at the Valley Manufacturing Company, where half of the employees are Russian "Old Believers."

"To say I was welcome would really be stretching it. I was tolerated... barely. One refused to let me take his picture, the others grudgingly allowed it. They spoke little English, and I quickly knew it was best to be as unobtrusive as possible. The light was terrible and I was forced to push my film to 1600 ASA; a strobe was out of the question," Cannefax wrote in her journal.

"I wanted to capture the flavor of this shop, to give a feeling of just how dark and old it really was. The 'Old Believers' seemed to fit these surroundings perfectly. In fact, if it weren't for the little modern touches like a baseball cap, one might feel they have stepped back in time," she concluded.

The human elements explored in this chapter illuminate basic themes. These photographs demonstrate with clarity that understanding people and social relationships does come from the work of photographers.

60. SALEM / 10:00 AM / MICHAEL
LLOYD

60. After a grueling session of arguments
over property tax relief legislation, Governor Victor Atiyeh takes time out to advise
House Speaker Grattan Kerans and Senate
President Ed Fadeley to adjourn the session
immediately. Friction between the two
leaders and their respective houses on the
sensitive issue had reached an all-time
high.

60

61. MCMINNVILLE / 10:30 AM / TOM BALLARD

62. HILLSBORO / 12:15 PM / MICHAL THOMPSON

63. NEAR HERMISTON / 10:50 AM / MICHAEL PARKER

61. Memories of Sunday drives and street "cruising" join the DeSotos, Chevrolets, Fords and Pontiacs in this junkyard's shredding machines. The shredder separates ferrous and non-ferrous metals, discarding glass and plastic.

62. At the Washington County Courthouse Complex in Hillsboro, Libertarian Party followers protest the imprisonment of a man who refused to comply with a local land-use ordinance. Protestors support the premise that the imprisoned man's constitutional right to use his property in any peaceful way he chooses has been violated.

63. An aerial photographer's interest is captured by the methodical designs created by a farmer. "A farmer is oblivious to the beautiful pattern he is making on the landscape."

61

63

62

64. SALEM / 10:30 AM / DEAN J. KOEPFLER

64. A six-by-eight-foot cell, equipped with only a sink, toilet and springless bed, offers this Oregon State Correctional Institution inmate few points of interest; he reads the comics as part of his usual midmorning routine.

64

65. Denzo, a member of the Hoedads treeplanting co-op explains that it is unusual for planting to be going on in July. Wet, cool weather had extended the season. The Hoedads say they are the best planters around, but competition from private contractors is making things tough on cooperatives.

66. Don Howary of Portland contemplates his garden, one of the biggest gardens in his Bonny Slope neighborhood.

65

66

67. CAMP SHERMAN / 12:30 PM / BOB ELLIS

68. MCMINNVILLE / 12:10 PM / TOM BALLARD

67. Bottoms up! Kids at Camp Sherman investigate the lunchtime activities of fish in the Metolius River.

68. Sam Jones begins laying bricks for a new ladle at the Cascade Steel Company which will hold 30,000 lbs. of molten steel.

67

68

69. ALBANY / 12:15 PM / BILL HUNTER

70. MCMINNVILLE / 11:20 AM / TOM BALLARD

69. Frank Cray of Teledyne Wah Chang keeps his distance while grinding the oxidation off a hot zirconium ingot.

70. Working with primary or fabricated metals demands complete concentration to avoid dangerous accidents. Larry Snyder of Cascade Steel Company cautiously clears debris near a ladle of molten metal.

70

69

71. PINE CREEK AREA / 11:30 AM /
     KEVIN CLARK

72. PINE CREEK AREA / 11:30 AM /
     KEVIN CLARK

71. Kathleen McFarlane does the brand-
ing while Bill Cobb holds the cow still. Don
McFarlane, Kathleen's husband, has
owned the ranch for 48 years.

72. Charles Conlee, 76, talks about his life
while taking a break from roping cows at
the McFarlane Ranch. Conlee was born and
has lived his whole life in the same house.

71

72

73. TROUTDALE / 11:45 AM / CHERYL K. BLANKENSHIP

74. COLUMBIA RIVER / 11:20 AM / MICHAEL HINSDALE

73. Claude Wright (who lives in a trailer in Boring) says that selling fruit from the back of a truck is a good way to meet people and reap the benefits of their knowledge. Despite the fact that he had yet to sell any fruit, he said, "It helps me to learn, to talk to people. I don't really care if I sell anything." He has set up his business this day in Troutdale.

74. Knappton tugboats guide a log raft along the Columbia River to the Port of Astoria and an awaiting Japanese ship. The nearly empty passageway reflects the recession's impact on the Pacific Northwest's shipping and logging industries.

74

73

75. NEAR ECHO / 11:00 AM / ROBERT PENNELL

76. LAKEVIEW / 12:45 PM / J.L. CLARK

77. WOODBURN / 10:45 AM / JILL A. CANNEFAX

75. Protective eyewear from the past takes on a New Wave look in the 1980s. Wray Hawkins, Sr., protects his eyes from the dust created while driving an older open-air tractor in Umatilla County.

76. Waiting for a mechanic to finish fixing your car feels like an eternity, until you start thinking about the bill. Lakeview residents Ron Garrison (left) and Carl Crawford wait for a gas station mechanic's final words on the subject. Garrison is a logger and Crawford makes moulding.

77. "Old Believer" Foma Cheruischov, a Russian immigrant living in Woodburn, keeps a wary eye on the photographer. His Old Believers community has maintained its Russian culture and social structure in spite of the 20th-century lifestyle surrounding them.

75

76

77

78. PORTLAND / 11:00 AM / BARBARA F. GUNDLE

79. EUGENE / 11:30 AM / DAN BATES

78. An elderly woman prepares for company in her room at Portland's Robison Home for the Aged.

79. Two-year-old Michael Spiller maintains a firm hold on his favorite stuffed animal and suitcase during his arrival in Eugene. Michael has come from Placerville, California on an Amtrak train to visit his grandmother in Eugene.

79

78

80. HILLSBORO / 11:00 AM / MICHAL THOMPSON

81. PORTLAND / 1:35 PM / MARY VOLM

80. Fourteen-month-old Kristopher Brester receives his first haircut from the experienced hands of Wess Hebron. Hebron has trimmed, shaped and styled hair for 25 years.

81. Fruit and Flower Child Care Center children exchange laughter during an outing to Laurelhurst Park in Portland.

80

81

82. Capturing the fleeting moments of childhood takes on new meaning when combined with the wide variety of cultures alive in Oregon. Ada Patrick, 78, gently rocks her seven-month-old grandson, Burke Sundown Farrow, in the quiet of her house on the Umatilla Indian Reservation.

83. Mother and daughter from the Ayhan family, who live in the Russian Old Believer village outside of Woodburn, relax during a rare session with a photographer.

84. Alongside the small lake at Portland's Laurelhurst Park, a child from the Fruit and Flower Child Care Center receives a lesson on behavior from a supervisor.

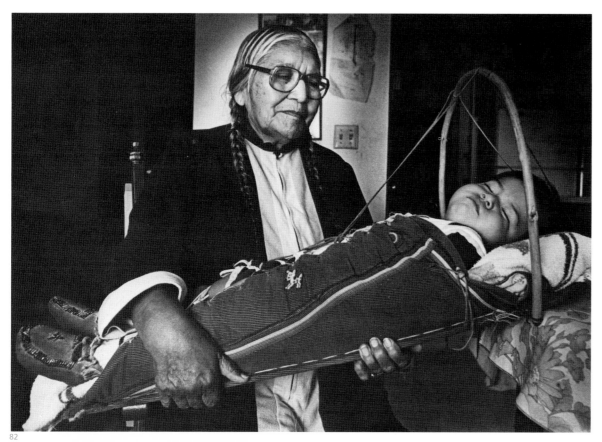

82

84

83

85. SALEM / 11:00 AM / DEE ANN HALL

86. SALEM / 11:40 AM / MICHAEL LLOYD

85. Capitol press corps members, from left, Don Jepsen (*Oregonian*), Paul Hansen and Stephanie Fowler (from Portland's Channels 2 and 6 respectively) exchange stories while awaiting Governor Victor Atiyeh's morning press conference.

86. In the governor's ceremonial office, Governor Victor Atiyeh reveals to the press his opinion that if property tax relief legislation is not passed before the regular session is over, he will schedule a special session in August.

85

86

ONE AVERAGE DAY

87. SALEM / 11:45 AM / DEAN J. KOEPFLER

88. NEAR WASCO / 11:30 AM / C. BRUCE FORSTER

87. An inmate at Salem's Oregon State Penitentiary has time on his hands. For causing trouble, he has been stripped of all privileges except for either a shower or a half-hour-a-day-walk in front of his cell.

88. Rancher Larry Kaseberg examines a single grain of wheat amidst millions at the Kaseberg Wheatacres Ranch in Wasco.

88

87

89.   NEAR FIVE RIVERS / 2:15 PM / JOHN BRAGG

90.   EUGENE / 12:30 PM / DAN BATES

89.   Gerald Smallwood, 28, takes a break from working with his five brothers on a log landing in the Siuslaw National Forest. Smallwood said he works in the family business because he earns more money than he would in a forest management position.

90.   Unemployed persons fill their stomachs' needs at the Eugene Mission.

89

90

91. PORTLAND / 12:20 PM / STEVE
BLOCH

91. Lunchtime for the construction workers laboring on the light rail project along
Portland's Banfield Freeway (I-84).

91

92. "Doc" Feves, a Pendleton physician, watches a backroom card game at Club Cigar Restaurant in Pendleton. The card games have been a local tradition for many years and continue throughout the day with few breaks.

93. South Bend, Washington residents Orion Carlisle, Darrell Thumm, and Marc Wilson (left to right) are captivated by a video game in a Seaside arcade. The boys were visiting the town on a field trip from a soccer camp in South Bend.

92

93

94.   Signs in Wallowa. "You can get lost in Lostine, you can enter Enterprise; you probably can get drunk on the Whiskey Creek Road, and a toper (archaic "tope") is a drunkard." Mere coincidence however, as Tope Creek was named for a 19th-century homesteader named William A. Tope.

95.   While best known for its mountains and forests, much of Oregon is open, with sparse vegetation. Here, a loaded pickup rushes along a dirt road in Lake County.

96.   After hitchhiking through California and Oregon, Jay Mead, a school teacher from New Hampshire, catches a ride from Lostine to Enterprise.

94

95

96

97. COLUMBIA GORGE / 1:20 PM / STEVE BLOCH

97. In spite of gray skies and relatively cool weather, a couple takes advantage of the local rules which allow nudity at Rooster Rock State Park.

97

98. Just a few miles upriver from the strolling couple (opposite), an Oregon City sturgeon fisherman checks his line at the outflow of Bonneville Dam.

98

99. PORTLAND / 12:30 PM / MARV BONDAROWICZ

100. SEASIDE / 1:10 PM / BILL WAGNER

101. PORTLAND / 12:40 PM / ROSS HAMILTON

99. Oregon's nearly constant pattering of showers often drives newcomers and residents alike nuts. Visiting conventioneers Carl Bybee of Eugene and New Yorker Ted Thompson (right) demonstrate the invaluable skill of being able to turn almost anything into a substitute umbrella.

100. A sudden downpour at Seaside finds Bruce Laughman using his kite as a short-term umbrella while Ray Pohl and his son, Nathan, attempt to ignore the rain.

101. Some Portland businessmen would feel naked without the prerequisite compact umbrella, which can be easily stashed in an attache case. Chuck Pagani, Gary Marx and David Dowell (left to right) stand at a street corner, conversing their lunch hour away.

99

100

101

102.   After transporting the animals from barns at Delta Park, mounted policeman Tom Peavey prepares Rebel and Doc for the start of their ten-hour shift in downtown Portland.

103.   Rasta, a well-known dog in Portland's vibrant northwest area, keeps flower seller Ellen Whiteside company. Rasta and Whiteside have worked at the same location for 19 months, through rain and sunshine.

104.   Baby elephants at play at Portland's Washington Park Zoo. They are part of a world-famous collection of elephants.

102

103

104

105. Main Street, Wallowa. This small town depends on the summer tourist trade. In this view, the street seems to be dominated by inducements for food and beverages.

106. Outside Antelope, at Rajneeshpuram, stands "Zarathustra Fields," one of three massive tent cities that provided shelter and cafeterias for part of the fifteen thousand followers of the community's guru at the Rajneesh Festival two weeks earlier.

105

106

107. NEAR PENDLETON / 1:15 PM / MICHAEL PARKER

108. PORTLAND / 11:20 AM / GEOFF PARKS

107. An early mission school for Indians and its cemetery offers a glimpse of one of Oregon's remaining historic relics.

108. The relics of Portland's history are shadowed and usually hidden by the constantly changing commercial interests in the downtown area. The early-20th-century tower of the First Congregational Church is dominated by the height of the Georgia Pacific Building (left) and the contemporary style of the mirrored Orbanco Building.

107

108

ONE AVERAGE DAY

109. BONNEVILLE DAM / 12:15 PM / BETH CAMPBELL

110. ALBANY / 12:40 PM / BILL HUNTER

111. BONNEVILLE DAM / 12:00 PM / BETH CAMPBELL

109. The mysteries of high technology remain intact at the fully automated Bonneville Dam. Humans are used to monitor the system, but usually remain unseen. While the photographer was in the structure, a ringing alarm on the power control panel summoned a technician who quietly appeared and then disappeared seated on an electric cart.

110. At Albany's Teledyne Wah Chang Company, an employee follows the multi-step process of drawing a 2½-inch zirconium rod down to ¼ inch. The machines are capable of drawing the wires to the width of a human hair.

111. At Bonneville Dam a row of generators at the recently completed power house are moved by 3,744 tons of water each second. This second Bonneville powerhouse was dedicated just two weeks earlier.

109

110

111

112. PORTLAND / 1:00 PM / BARBARA F. GUNDLE

113. COOS BAY / 1:45 PM / BRUCE W. SMITH

114. BALD MOUNTAIN / 12:00 PM / S. JOHN COLLINS

112. From within the center of Portland's U.S. Bank Tower to a mine at Bald Mountain, the corps of Oregon's work force is found at places not usually listed on a tourist's map. Barbara Walters, the first woman steamfitter in the state, diligently threads a pipe in the U.S. Bank's new highrise headquarters.

113. Paul Ehrlich sprays paint onto the hull of a ship at Coos Bay's Mid-Coast Marine Company. When it is completed the vessel will be bound for Alaska.

114. Joel W. Jeffery, Ibex Mining Company geologist, examines a quartz-rich sediment sample for gold at the Bald Mountain laboratory.

112

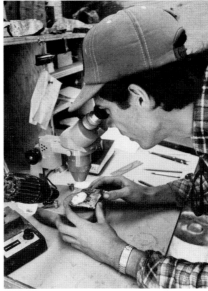

114

113

115. GLENWOOD / 1:00 PM / MICHAL THOMPSON

116. SEASIDE / 12:30 PM / BILL WAGNER

115. At Washington County's Gales Creek Children's Camp, mail call features an unusual tradition; anyone receiving more than four pieces of mail is guaranteed an involuntary dip in the swimming pool.

116. Sibling rivalry stimulated a swinging broadjump competition at Seaside between Jay (background) and Joel Belgarde, while sisters Merriann and Mandy watch. The Belgardes are from Canby.

115

116

117. LAKEVIEW / 1:25 PM / J. L. CLARK

118. BETWEEN BURNS AND HINES / 1:15 PM / KEITH SKELTON

119. PORTLAND / 10:30 AM / ROSS HAMILTON

117. Lakeview police chief Troy Riblett (left) with fireman and dispatcher Gene Hollingshead watch for all midday emergencies from the dispatcher's room in the town's fire station.

118. Cherie McKirdy, the youngest of 10 children, strikes a pose in front of her parents' home, which stands at the border between Hines and Burns.

119. A group of Japanese art students visiting Portland asked Portlander Sue York to take a picture of them in front of Michael Graves' Portland Building.

117

118

119

DAYTON / 3:00 PM / JILL A. CANNEFAX

ELGIN / 2:30 PM / DAVID WEINTRAUB

NEAR HEPPNER / 4:00 PM / MICHAEL PARKER

SMITH ROCK / 1:45 PM / DAN BASTIAN

Turkeys at Charlie Ever's farm near Dayton (top left), are part of the 800,000 of the fowl raised each year in Yamhill County. These birds are about to be shipped to the Norbest plant in Salem.

Budweiser, Oly and Red Baron Pizza can be purchased at this establishment in Elgin (bottom left). The rodeo and other attractions associated with the Elgin Stampede are in full swing, and the photographer turns away from a street full of vendors, shoppers and onlookers to take this view.

During a flight from Pendleton to Madras, aerial photographer Michael Parker focused his camera on this lovely field pattern east of Heppner (bottom center), one of many such designs on the face of the Deschutes-Umatilla Plateau.

A lone climber scaling Smith Rock (right). This 3,200 foot ridge at a bend of the Crooked River is part of Smith Rock State Park just east of U.S. Highway 97, north of Redmond.

4
AFTERNOON

Sundown comes late on a summer day. This is good, because there are so many things to do, and the additional time of light offers the opportunity to accomplish them. If you work, the days can drone by slowly. In an office, air-conditioned during the summer, you are lucky not to have windows which reveal to you just how much beauty is passing with each hour. If you are outside, the days are overpowering gestures of nature's munificence. Everyone's heart yearns for escape. In that sense, any beautiful day when you are working is a long haul.

To be out and about and playing when it is summertime is also a long haul, but much nicer. Tourists are wandering about Oregon in the summer, millions of them. They look over the shoulders of Oregonians and snap pictures of the state's waterfalls and scenery. Sometimes it seems as if there are too many visitors, but they are cultivated as are wheat, timber, berries, cattle and fish.

While a prison inmate lifts weights and fills his time, Oregon politicians face and (in some cases) deflect weighty problems for the regular session of the Oregon legislature—two more forms of the long haul.

Perhaps the longest haul of all is pulled by those who go out to watch the rest of us fill our day—photojournalists and freelancers. Their summer days, indoors and out, are recorded in this chapter. On the afternoon of 15 July 1983, the more than ninety photographers watched people through their cameras' eyes and Oregon was looked at from everywhere; from Burns, where you can throw a rock and not hit anything but another rock, to Portland's Transit Mall, where police on horseback are not an anachronism.

Start out about 2:30 PM and go to the Five O'Clock News. Maybe a big lunch, one coffee break and then, work. One man rides aboard a tractor. He tills 30 acres in one day. What does he think about? When does he "feel" the day begin to end?

There is an amazing abundance of modes of transportation in this section. There are "classic" American covered wagons and "articulated" buses from Hungary, there are ferries, gillnetters' and tour boats, airliners and rescue planes, firetrucks and ATVs (used for both ranching and recreation), there are tractors and wheelchairs, Rolls Royces and abandoned pickups. One man transports himself up a rock wall.

A champion draws the string on her bow, a youngster holds a play pistol and there are real rockets. Some of the persons shown here are sunning themselves, others are just sitting.

There is wheat. Will that good wheat eventually become part of a meal at Bernie Hannaford's Hines Cafe, which proudly advertises the "Worst Food in Oregon"? Hannaford, photographed by Keith Skelton, has gained national fame: the *Wall Street Journal,* "Good Morning America," "Real People" and others have seen fit to do features on the man who says, "Come and get hospitalized!"

In Kevin Clark's photograph, the Bible is open to the First Book of the Kings and Audrey and Jim Anderson are home in the little church in Lone Rock, a long haul from their real home in Beaverton. So when does the Bhagwan come? At 2:00 PM, a Rolls Royce is driven slowly by the homage of "blissed out" Sannyasins, dressed in pink or red or shades of orange, arrayed in the colors of the sun.

Waiting is a long haul. There are those who wait for the good old times to come back and are disappointed. There are those who wait for the fast rush of a new trend—and they are disappointed too. Can anyone say it is wrong to own only a tent, a television and a parrot?

Why did Harvey and Anita Senter get that store back on its feet in Bellfountain, then contemplate to move again? A long haul, as with waiting for your laundry, or a haircut, or a mood; perhaps an experience you have never had before.

We will go there and we will talk or listen; we will pull the long haul and then we will sit and wait for the sun to go down late and slow as it does in summer.

120. CROWN POINT / 2:00 PM /
STEVE BLOCH

121. MULTNOMAH FALLS /
2:30 PM / STEVE BLOCH

120. At Crown Point, near the western end of the Gorge, this family forms a tableau against the typically Oregon backdrop of clouds, forested hills and the Columbia River. The Gorge is the state's most-visited tourist site.

121. It is the favorite tourist attraction in Oregon—the Columbia River Gorge and its accompanying attributes. Countless rolls of film are exposed here — part of the compulsion to record one's visit to a famous place. Probably the most visited spot in the Gorge is Multnomah Falls, and here a gentleman poses on this gray July day.

120

121

122. So you want to be a farmer? Then you have to learn to till 30 acres in a day. Reiner Benting, 59, of Eugene, does just that; he always does it with a cheek full of chewing tobacco. Here Benting takes a break and shows off the mileage on his "OshKosh B'Gosh" overalls.

122

123. NEAR HERMISTON / 2:30 PM / STEVE NEHL

124. PRINCETON / 2:00 PM / GREGORY J. LAWLER

123. Several hundred miles north of Benjy, Howard King handles 90 mm shells, replacing fuses at the Umatilla Army Ordnance Depot.

124. Playfully pointing a water pistol at himself, is six-year-old Benjy Davis, who lives in the Harney County town of Princeton.

123

124

125. JORDAN VALLEY / 2:30 PM /
DAVE SWAN

125. A solitary woman sits silhouetted amidst tall memorials in this Jordan Valley cemetery. The memorial flowers are plastic because, the woman said, "We had a killing frost just last night." Photographer Dave Swan notes, "It seems as if everything sits silhouetted against the horizon in eastern Oregon."

125

126. Gary Brown and Jerry McKee, wearing protective gear, begin to inspect rockets stored at the Umatilla Army Depot, looking for any contamination or leakage.

126

127. NEAR HERMISTON / 2:00 PM / STEVE NEHL

128. NEAR HERMISTON / 2:15 PM / STEVE NEHL

127. Before entering the Umatilla Army Depot's dangerous chemical storage area, employee Jerry McKee suits up.

128. Despite its menacing purpose — storing arms — the depot still is a place where the antelope can play. The Umatilla Army Depot is also an animal preserve, and over two hundred antelope live in the fields surrounding the storage buildings.

128

127

129. SALEM / 2:30 PM / MICHAEL
LLOYD

130. SALEM / 2:45 PM / MICHAEL
LLOYD

129. During the long hours of waiting around on this the last day of the 62nd Oregon Legislative Assembly, a very serious Tom Throop, state representative from Bend, scans a newspaper, his prayerful attitude perhaps indicating his feelings about any special sessions the governor might call after the legislature's last day.

130. Meanwhile, Representative Vera Katz, whose district is a portion of Portland, shows the fatigue of the last lingering day of the session.

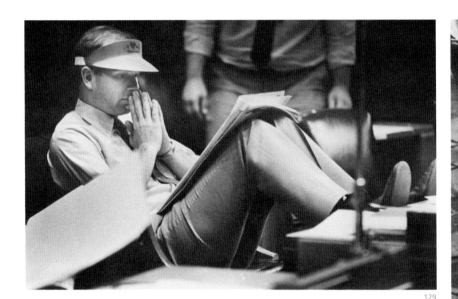

129

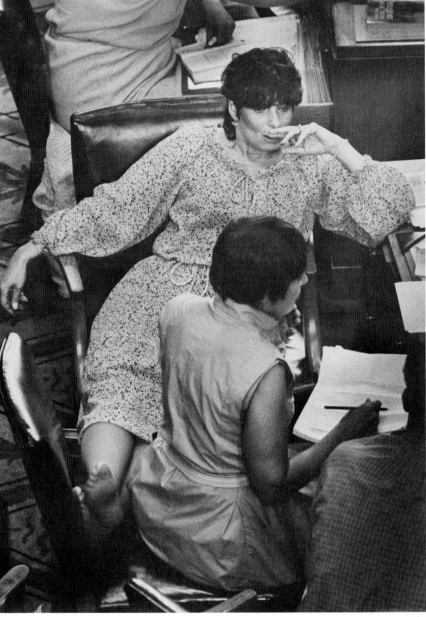

130

131.   Sometimes, when you are the mayor
of Portland, things are like that — a bridge
to open, a freeway to close, a funny hat to
wear, another plaque on the wall — then
comes a personal time; here Frank Ivancie
takes time to talk on the phone with someone in his family.

131

132. SALEM / 2:20 PM / DEAN J. KOEPFLER

133. PENDLETON / 3:00 PM / ROBERT PENNELL

132. An Oregon State Penitentiary inmate "pumps iron" in a part of the main exercise yard, a part referred to as the "pile yard."

133. Jim Ralph (right) an aide at Eastern Oregon State Hospital in Pendleton, comforts a protectively masked patient at the hospital. Jim will lose his job if plans to convert the hospital to a prison become a reality.

132

133

134. PORTLAND / 2:00 PM / RAE CAREY

135. SUMPTER / 2:30 PM / RICH IWASAKI

134. Waiting for something to happen outside a Portland record store, Gabrielle Drinard (left) and Courtenay Stelljes, students at Cleveland High School, grab a smoke on this midsummer Friday afternoon.

135. Vi and O.B. Munger, who have just stopped in for an ice cream at One-Eyed Charlie's Cafe in Sumpter, live most of each year in North Powder, and have a summer place here near this old northeastern Oregon mining town.

135

134

136. Historically, Oregon has been a place to move to. The early pioneers crossed the plains in wagons to find new lives, land and freedom in Oregon. Expressing themselves in a "traditional" way are 4-H horse club members from Tillamook and Washington counties, trekking on Bayocean Peninsula to celebrate "Breakaway '83." The group had 9 wagons, 50 saddle horses and 10 teams of draft horses to carry 150 "pioneers," ages 7 to 79.

137. In another part of the state — at Rajneeshpuram, pioneers of a less "traditional" sort and followers of the Bhagwan Shree Rajneesh, greet their leader during his daily rounds in his "wagon," one of 30 bullet-proof Rolls Royces owned by the Bhagwan. The Rajneesh claim they are seeking many of the same things as their 19th-century predecessors.

136

137

138. PORTLAND / 2:00 PM / CLAUDIA
J. HOWELL

139. BEND / 3:15 PM / DAN BASTIAN

138. Mounted policeman Robert Moser
(left) on his horse Doc, and Tom Peavy on
Rebel confront the present, in the form of a
Hungarian-made "articulated bus," from
seats in the past. They are patrolling Portland's Transit Mall, where the future will
bring light rail.

139. An older form of transportation still
popular is hitchhiking, or "goosing the
ghost," here being practiced successfully
by Jim Arata, 22, of Bend. Arata is pictured
here endeavoring to hitch out of Bend,
"the first ride out of town is the hardest,"
seeking a lift to Grants Pass. In the past,
the same trip had taken Jim six hours to
thumb.

138

139

140. LAKE COUNTY / 2:00 PM / DALE SWANSON

140. Completing an S-curve in the vastness of southeastern Oregon's Lake County, a lone vehicle throws up a rooster tail of dust as it moves into what could be described as "nowhere."

140

141. COBURG / 2:15 PM / BETTY UDESEN

142. MILLER ISLAND / 2:30 PM / C. BRUCE FORSTER

141. Reiner Benting (see photograph 122) moves his tractor across this Lane County field near Coburg, creating a pattern on the land.

142. Irrigation piping being used on Miller Island in the Columbia River near the mouth of the Deschutes River. Miller Island is near Miller, Oregon, and is often mistakenly thought to be in Oregon, even by native Oregonians. Actually the island is in Klickitat County, Washington.

141

142

ONE AVERAGE DAY

143. Happier for the experience, a file of followers of the Bhagwan Shree Rajneesh experience a sense of bliss after sharing a view of the Bhagwan during his daily rounds at their newly built community in Wasco County.

144. No one in Burns could pronounce for the photographer the name of this old church on the Burns Paiute Indian Reservation. A young man had just finished cutting the lawn as the photographer arrived.

145. Caretakers of this fine old church in Lonerock are Audrey and Jim Anderson, who commute here on weekends from their home in Beaverton. The building dates from 1898, and the Andersons have recently taken it upon themselves to maintain it.

143

144

145

146. For Emory Mathews, a Lonerock resident in his seventies, his waiting will not open the Lonerock Store, which closed in the 1960s after more than one-half-century of business. Mathews has lived in this small town since his grade school days.

147. For Tony Chic, however, idling on a summer afternoon outside downtown Portland's Rock 'n Roll Fashions, waiting along Park Avenue is what you do until something happens.

147

146

148. Rodney Scoggins is "making do." The 23-year-old man has no job and recently split with his wife. He has a tarp, tent, refrigerator (which is empty), his television and some additional personal belongings. He uses the bathroom and shower in his sister-in-law's house, too crowded with five persons for him to live inside. "I enjoy it," he says, "I'm not sure I'd do anything differently if I were working."

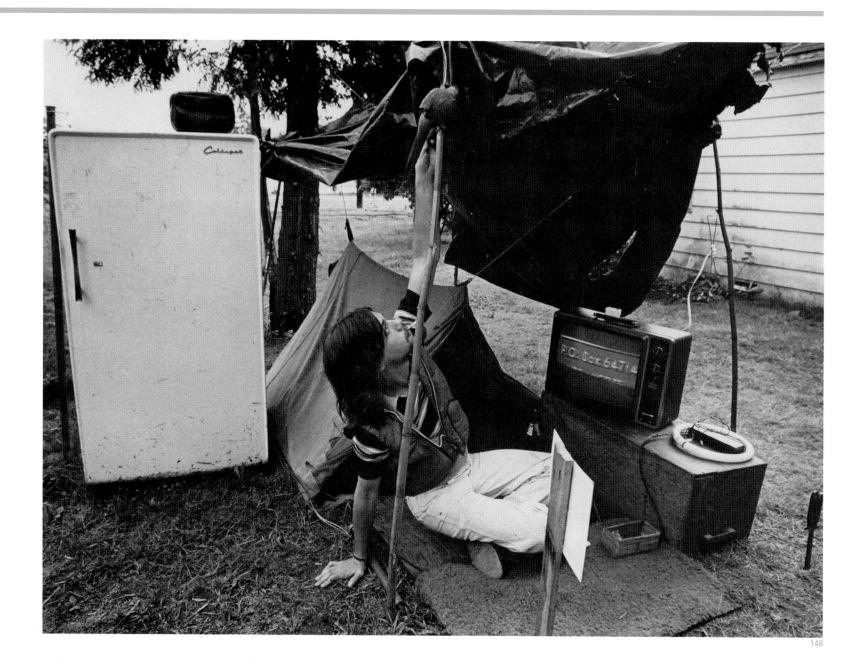

148

149. LAKE OSWEGO / 3:00 PM /
STEVE DiPAOLA

149. Judy and Pete Kershaw have done
well. You might say their success has been
the result of "sharp practices" — their
sports knife business bought this Lake
Oswego home, their 1957 Rolls Royce and
brought the smiles to their faces.

149

150. KAH-NEE-TA / 3:33 PM /
MARSHA SHEWCZYK

151. LAKEVIEW / 3:00 PM / J. L. CLARK

152. COLUMBIA RIVER / 3:35 PM /
BETH CAMPBELL

150. Hoping for luscious tans, these women are soaking up the sun at Kah-Nee-Ta Resort on the Warm Springs Indian Reservation in central Oregon. Here, they say, there is sunshine 360 days of the year.

151. Hitting that little white ball around on the rural links at Lakeview Golf Course is Bud Williams, a retired employee from the Pacific Power & Light Co. He and his wife have taken up golfing together.

152. Millicent and Charles Bennett, of Medford (left), enjoy the sights along the Columbia River Gorge aboard a tour boat that picks up tourists on the Oregon side at Bonneville Dam, Cascade Locks and Stevenson, Washington. Their shipmates, Bernie and Janet Bober (right), on vacation in the West, take this relaxing river ride.

150

151

152

153. RAJNEESHPURAM /
3:15 PM / RANDY WOOD

154. PORTLAND / 2:00 PM / RANDY L.
RASMUSSEN

153. No matter how idyllic it may seem, Rajneeshpuram is no safer from fire than anywhere else. Swami Antar Samira stands in front of the community's firehouse and its gently humorous admonition of danger. Of course, the fire engine is red.

154. Kevin Muilenburg, 10, who did not pay enough attention to the danger of fire, is carefully removed from an Emanuel Hospital Lifeflight aircraft for transportation to the Portland hospital's burn center. The boy, injured after tossing gasoline on a fire in Cove, Oregon, is loaded by nurse Pat Roberg and pilot Mark Hohstadt, while his parents, Mary Jane and Bill Muilenberg, remove belongings from the plane.

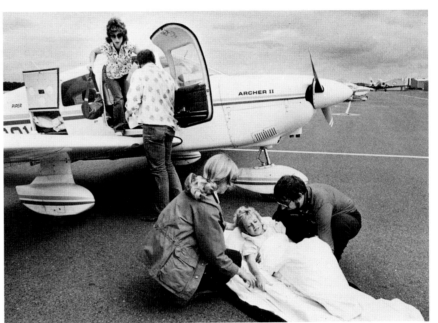

154

153

155. NEAR WASCO / 4:30 PM / C. BRUCE FORSTER

156. NEAR WASCO / 4:30 PM / C. BRUCE FORSTER

157. NEAR WASCO / 5:30 PM / C. BRUCE FORSTER

155. Sherry Kaseberg and the family dog, Gray (on one of the family's twelve Honda motorcycles), return from inspecting the wheat.

156. Kevin Kaseberg operates a Wheatacres Ranch combine to cut a test swatch of the wheat. This test will determine the moisture content of the crop.

157. Sherman County is wheat country. The crop, at times, is like a vast golden inland sea unto itself. Farming families thrive on growing wheat so that families around the nation (and the world) can thrive on bread. Here is an aerial view of a country road on the east edge of the Kaseberg family's Wheatacres Ranch near Wasco.

155

156

157

158. Bernie Hannaford says he is only being honest in admitting that he serves the worst food in Oregon. For some restaurateurs, a similar expression of bravado would bring a visit from the health official. But for Hannaford, whose restaurant is in Hines, outside of Burns, this advertising has brought him world-wide renown. "Come in and get hospitalized!" is a familiar Hannaford challenge.

158

159. BELLFOUNTAIN / 3:45 PM / JOHN BRAGG

160. BURNS / 2:30 PM / KEITH SKELTON

159. Harvey and Anita Senter came up to Bellfountain from California seven years ago, and turned a no-money, falling-down gas pump operation into the flourishing Bellfountain Market. "It takes money to make money," says Harvey, who is now thinking of selling the whole thing to do some traveling.

160. The photographer drops in at Bob Hebener's 2nd Hand Store in Burns and is asked if he is trying to sell his cameras. Bob (in baseball hat), Harvey Hamilton (cowboy hat), Laverne Hebener and son Peter all have a great sense of humor, so grab a cup of coffee and sit a spell.

159

160

161. Blindfolded follower of the Bhagwan Shree Rajneesh takes time for peace
and solitude in the two-acre Buddha Hall
at Rajneeshpuram in central Oregon.

161

162. BURNS / 4:00 PM / GREGORY
J. LAWLER

162. Held in an aspic of ennui, denizens
of a Burns laundromat contemplate a late
afternoon's drying and folding while the
rest of the world . . . washes, perhaps.

162

163. BONNY SLOPE / 4:15 PM / JOHN MAHER

164. PORTLAND / 4:00 PM / CATHY CHENEY

163. This old-fashioned one-chair barber shop in Bonny Slope (in the hills just west of Portland) is a quaint anachronism. This establishment (recently reopened) is run by the grandson of the original barber.

164. At his studio in Portland, Mark Rabiner works with model Lisa Sinclair's hair in order to capture the look he has envisioned.

164

163

165. NEAR BROWNSMEADE /
4:45 PM / DANA OLSEN

166. KNAPPA / 4:30 PM / DANA
OLSEN

165. Gillnet fishermen's fish coop on
Gnat Creek tide waters near Brownsmeade
looks still, serene and uninhabited in the
late afternoon light.

166. A 1959 Ford pickup sits in an old
garage belonging to Kewpie Ziak on Gnat
Creek Road, near Knappa. The displayed
antler collection spans 50 years.

165

166

167. WINCHESTER BAY / 5:30 PM / BRUCE W. SMITH

168. CANNON BEACH / 4:30 PM / BILL WAGNER

169. SHERWOOD / 4:30 PM / JIM THOMPSON

167. John Nunn rides his ATV, a Honda 250 three-wheeler, across the sandy open spaces of the Oregon Dunes National Recreation Area, near Umpqua Lighthouse. Nunn is an independent building contractor in Reedsport, who loves to "roost-it" whenever he can.

168. On the stunning Oregon coast, at Cannon Beach near the mouth of Ecola Creek, several horseback riders enjoy the surf.

169. Carolyn Phillips practices at a Sherwood Archery range for the National Field Archery Association Championship (competition was scheduled for 25-26 July 1983 in Watkins Glen, New York, where Phillips did win the national title, breaking the old record by 186 points).

167

168

169

170. WESTPORT / 4:35 PM / MICHAEL HINSDALE

171. PORTLAND / 4:25 PM / CLAUDIA J. HOWELL

170. The last ferry that crosses the Columbia River in Oregon, this one travels between the Clatsop County town of Westport and Puget Island. These cars, trucks and tour bus are traveling toward Cathlamet, across the island and in Washington.

171. One man from a maintenance crew washes windows, preparing flight 1289 for a non-stop to Los Angeles. Stationed at Gate 41 this United Airlines plane is one of many that connect Portland International Airport with the rest of the nation.

170

171

172. PORTLAND / 4:45 PM / RANDY
 RASMUSSEN

173. PORTLAND / 5:15 PM / MAURY
 DAHLEN

174. PORTLAND / 4:30 PM / MAURY
 DAHLEN

172. Choices about the news that you read and see have to be made somewhere, choices made by people who try to decide on the best presentation of the news. At the *Oregonian*, news and photograph editors gather each day with Executive Editor William Hilliard (center, facing) for the daily "prayer meeting." The meeting will determine the news, photographs and features of coming editions, and how they will be presented in Oregon's largest daily.

173. The edited story will appear on either this early evening newscast or the 11:00 PM version of KOIN news. Newscasters Mike Donahue and Judy Rooks (about to deliver an introduction to a story on crop damage resulting from the heavy summer rainfall) are being directed here by Charlie Parr.

174. Similar decisions must be made about the news that is to appear on television. At almost the same time as the *Oregonian* meeting, KOIN staffers John Keller (left) and Wayne Faligowski edit a story shot that day about a temporary public heliport in Portland.

174

172

173

HOSMER LAKE / 6:30 PM / DAN BASTIAN

EUGENE / 5:30 PM / DAN BATES

WASHINGTON COUNTY / 6:00 PM / TERRY FARRIS

EUGENE / 5:40 PM / DAN BATES

NEAR SALEM / 5:00 PM / JILL CANNEFAX

EUGENE / 7:00 PM / WAYNE EASTBURN

Mt. Bachelor from Hosmer Lake, Deschutes County (top left). Hard at work on the other side of the peak are crews preparing a new ski lift to the top of the mountain.

A woman living in the University of Oregon Amazon Housing Project watches out her window on the evening of the 15th (top center). These housing units near South Eugene High School are provided by the University for married students.

Two couples (top right) enjoy an outdoor hot tub and wine during the evening at a Washington County nudist colony. On the deck in the background, and ironically covered up in a little cloth bag, is a dog.

A young couple (bottom left), with "punk" haircuts and dress, walk along Hilyard Street in the southern section of Eugene.

Located on Highway 221 is the Daum fruitstand (bottom right). Gary Daum, his wife and mother have had this family-run operation for 15 years.

Alberto Salazar leads the field and Ron Tabb (left) at an evening all-comers meet at the University of Oregon's Hayward Field (opposite page). Jim Hill eventually defeated local heroes Salazar and Tabb in a relatively slow 10,000 meters—recording a time of 27 minutes and 59.5 seconds.

ONE AVERAGE DAY

5
DUSK

In summer when the sun is still high, people often gather in the evening to contemplate the day, before the welcome coolness steals in with the promise of sleep.

Gatherings occur in many places. Some come to play, some to give birth, others to reflect upon a day that could be their last, a day in a "history of days," while others lie etherized as a surgeon repairs the damage to a tired heart.

Summer seems to give people the long evenings almost intentionally, for when we have cleaned away the hot tiredness and finished our meal, there is the luxury of languishing and looking—sittin' and starin'—a time for pure reflection, time to be spent on ourselves.

If you were to go out, as did the photographers whose images fill this chapter, and find people gathering and doing the evening, where would you begin? You could look where there are people or where there are not people. That is the beauty of a summer evening—it is open.

Evening can mean a corner basketball hoop, the YMCA gymnasium, a lake where monster-lunker trout threaten to break the surface and crackle a sunset reflection into a thousand shards of red, pink, gold and blue. Go on up to Greenhorn if you feel like it, to find an old man just gathering the past with his thoughts. In the city there is the flag flying and a man and woman are marrying beneath a cathedral of baseball bats.

The photographers brought back the evening hours of 15 July 1983 stuffed in film cans, hoping to record the dusk time and to help us recognize ourselves. In the desert and eastern high country they learned men could become "jackasses" voluntarily, or could be alone to reflect on more serious things. In crowded cities, they saw that the last of the day is shared as it is shared anywhere: a running trail, a hot spring which developers have left alone, a carnival, or alone in a library with books you can no longer read.

Most of all, if brought down to bed properly, summer evenings can be a gathering of the spirit; a time to collect the soul and remember how it was or is when we are young. The merging into twilight is a magic time. In that sense, it is a period refreshingly quiet, a pause that allows for gleaning of thoughts.

175. EUGENE / 5:30 PM / CHARLIE NYE

176. PORTLAND / 5:30 PM / BARBARA F. GUNDLE

177. PORTLAND / 6:25 PM / ROSS HAMILTON

175. Twirling her hair during a lull in the action, 10-year-old Cara Duncan waits for the softball to come her way at University Park ballfield in Eugene.

176. Getting in shape is moving, jumping, leaping, stretching—an aerobics class meets in the gym at the Portland Metro YMCA.

177. Slam dunking in a northeast Portland neighborhood. These friends enthusiastically allowed the photographer to capture their game on film. Perhaps a little *too* enthusiastically. By the time the game was over, the basketball hoop was detached from the backboard.

175

176

177

ONE AVERAGE DAY

178.	First-time attendants of the Hart Mountain Antelope Refuge are termed "Jackasses" by their fellow Antelopes. One neophyte brought along a t-shirt to match his new status.

179.	Warming himself at the barbecue fire during the annual get-together of the Order of the Antelope, Portland attorney Walter Martin counteracts a chill, as the sun drops to dusk at the 7,000-foot level of the Hart Mountain Antelope Refuge. The enormous fire will cook a whole steer over-night for all to enjoy.

180.	Lost in the reverie of rehearsing their music for competition, Herbert Hadley (left) of New Plymouth, Idaho, and Richard Steinger, of Letha, Idaho, pick and fiddle during the Blue Mountain Old Time Fiddlers' Contest in Baker.

178

179

180

181. WINSTON / 6:40 PM / LISA STONE

182. DAYTON / 5:05 PM / DEAN J. KOEPFLER

183. KINTON / 3:05 PM / CHRISTIE GRAY

184. JACKSONVILLE / 6:35 PM / ROB JAFFE

181. A popular tourist attraction in Oregon is Wildlife Safari at Winston. All of the animals roam freely over the rolling acres of open land in the park-like setting, with the predators kept separate. The man at the right is Otto Berosini, a well-known animal trainer, who performs in annual summer outdoor shows produced for visitors to the Safari. This Bengal tiger was raised by Berosini, as are all those in the "Otto Berosini's Exotic Cat Show."

182. Finding a dry spot on 15 July 1983 was next to impossible because the month was the second rainiest July on record for the State. But Timbo, in Dayton, found a spot for himself underneath the rear bumper of Floyd and Joann Osband's (his owners) car.

183. At Hesse Hog Farm in Kinton, Spiro Agnew mugs for the camera.

184. Goat-milking time in Applegate Valley. The cats know that a free squirt of fresh, warm milk will come their way if they have patience.

181

183

182

184

185. At the new Family Maternity Center of the Providence Medical Center in Portland, Diane Yazzolini takes her grandchildren Jason and Erin Mills out for a pizza dinner, after a visit to their parents and new-born brother, Jacob.

186. Meanwhile, in the birthing room, Keith and Janet Mills, the parents of Jason, Erin and newborn Jacob, enjoy a champagne and lobster dinner in celebration of the 2:00 AM birth. The catered family affair is a feature of the Family Maternity Center.

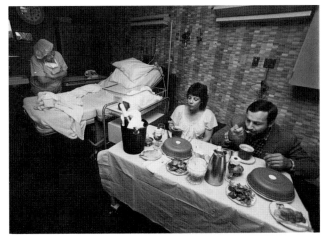

186

185

187.	CORVALLIS / 7:30 PM / TOM WARREN

188.	GREENHORN / 5:00 PM / S. JOHN COLLINS

187.	Harriet Moore, 87, retired Oregon State University archivist, battles frustration after recently being declared legally blind. Her first love is the study of Oregon history. Books on Oregon, as well as books by Oregon authors, line the walls of her living room. Today, however, she must use her ears rather than her eyes; compact cassette tapes are among her closest 'friends'.

188.	Guy Miller, 81, an old timer who has spent the past 10 summers in Greenhorn, acts as watchman or honorary policeman for the community, and is also a local living curiosity. Though his winters are spent quietly in Jacksonville, each summer Miller is a big—perhaps the only—tourist attraction in Greenhorn, where visitors usually sign the guest register, take a photograph of Guy and move on.

187

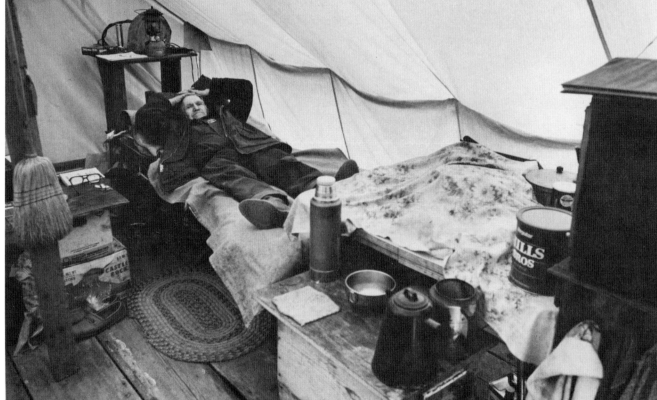

188

189. Two teenagers enjoy the "paratrooper" ride at a local carnival in Lakeview, sponsored by merchants to promote their "Crazy Day" Sale.

190. At McCredie Hot Springs, 10 miles east of Oakridge, Mike, Shervy and Tim (left to right) share the natural warmth of the spring. McCredie has been leased by the Forest Service to developers who plan a lodge and restaurant for the site. Oakridge residents have differing opinions concerning the development — some believe that an increase in tourist trade would result from it, but others object, saying, "It means you'll have to pay to come here."

191. Maggie Groos, a runner for Athletics West track club, sponsored by the Nike Corporation, passes by a fellow runner, who had decided to walk part of the way on the Amazon Trail in Eugene.

189

191

190

192. HOSMER LAKE / 6:30 PM / DAN BASTIAN

193. MALHEUR LAKE / 6:00 PM / GREGORY J. LAWLER

192. A fisherman on Hosmer Lake in the Cascades working hard at fly fishing. This lake is stocked with Atlantic salmon specifically for fly-fishermen, but once caught, the fish must be released immediately. The lake is a favorite haunt for the osprey, an eagle that dives into the lake after its prey. Fishermen report that it is not uncommon to catch a salmon with deep claw marks on its back.

193. Malheur Lake has flooded out neighboring homes and ranches. This is the worst flooding of the lake that anyone can recall in the last 50 years. There is no external drainage and so the area will remain flooded until the water evaporates.

192

193

106

194. TIGARD / 6:30 PM / SHAN
GORDON

195. APPLEGATE VALLEY / 6:30 PM /
ROBERT JAFFE

194. The march of suburbia takes over
the landscape as condominiums line
Scholls Ferry Road in Tigard.

195. On a high ridge in Applegate Valley,
B. Iverson has constructed this geodesic
dome. He and his family live here without
the benefit of outside electrical service and
their water is pumped by a 50-foot wind-
mill that Iverson welded and assembled
himself.

194

195

196. MAUPIN / 5:30 PM / RANDY
WOOD

197. SHERMAN COUNTY / 5:45 PM /
C. BRUCE FORSTER

196. City slickers are made to feel right at home at the Conroy Ranch, near Maupin. A little prairie humor is displayed here, providing people from the city a few appropriate urban conveniences such as this telephone and fire hydrant, which, of course, do not work.

197. Powerlines in Sherman County create a stark, somewhat abstract visual image. Seldom is the impact of technology on the land so startlingly apparent.

196

197

198.   George Singer, a 78-year-old retired Salem farmer considers this 1936 Chevy pickup, as well as two other Chevrolets and eleven Packards, his backup for Social Security. "I keep them around as an investment and they are worth more each year," he explained. Singer waits until the warmth of August and then starts up a few of the old engines to keep them in shape.

198

199. Ron Jukemich celebrates his 30th birthday with nurses in the Oncology Unit at Providence Medical Center in Portland. (Ron lived 42 more days before his cancer killed him.)

199

200. PORTLAND / 8:30 PM / ALAN
BORRUD

201. PORTLAND / 10:00 AM / ALAN
BORRUD

200. Cradling a pillow made by his wife, Roy Gochnour sleeps following open heart surgery.

201. A look at open-heart surgery. This is one of several bypasses performed on Roy Gochnour earlier in the day. A vein from his left leg was extracted and cut into lengths as needed for replacements in the heart. During the operation, his other leg was kept sterilized in order to save time, in case a second length of vein was needed.

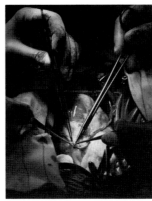

201

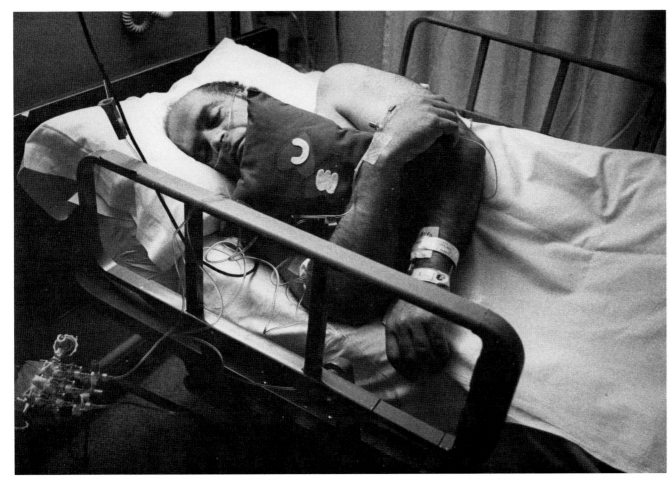

200

202. Josephine Crump (right) said this flag was given to her by a man a couple of years ago after he helped her get gas for her car. The man, she said, told her it was given to his family after his father died in World War II. Betty Huffman (left) and her son, David, and Monica Huffman and her son, Perry Jo, join Josephine in front of the "grand old flag."

202

203. Jamie Reynolds, who wanted to give his bride, Shery Otos, the biggest diamond he could find, asked the Portland Beavers baseball team to help the couple become man and wife at home plate at Portland Civic Stadium.

203

THE DALLES / 8:30 PM / STEVE NEHL

NEAR HARRISBURG / 9:00 PM / DAN BATES

BURNS / 9:15 PM / KEITH SKELTON

ASHLAND / 9:35 PM / CHRISTOPHER BRISCOE

As the evening turns to night, photographer Steve Nehl records — using a wide-angle lens — the beginning of this bareback rider's effort at The Dalles Rodeo (top left).

Just south of Harrisburg, along Coburg Road, a young girl has just finished hanging her family's wash (bottom left). Tired of urban living, her family had moved recently to this rural area north of Eugene.

Most small towns have a movie house — not all of them still in operation. The Desert Theater on Burns' main street (right) is showing the first-run feature, *Superman III*. The young woman selling tickets came across the street to ask why someone would set up their tripod and photograph her place of work, since, to her eyes, "it is so ugly!"

Two members of the Oregon Shakespearean Festival's production of *Cymbeline* capture the attention of an audience during a dramatic moment at a soldout performance of one of the Bard's last plays (opposite page).

6
NIGHT

Repeatedly, outsiders contemplating a move to Oregon say, "You have the beaches, the mountains and the desert. You have an expanding industrial base, and politically, the state is aggressive on many controversial issues. But what happens at night?"

Convincing these people that Oregonians do not all ride off into the sunset on Appaloosas, drinking Henry Weinhard's, and singing "Home on the Range" can be very difficult.

The easiest way to prove that Oregon is alive and well, even after the day is over, is to take them on a journey around the state and show them that life still continues at night.

The photographs in this chapter cover midevening to midnight, and the stories told here can be used as proof that, although it is past sunset, Oregonians do not disappear.

Political battles and interests do not end at sunset either. Michael Lloyd's telling photograph of a lobbyist (waiting in a pay telephone booth for the state legislature's session to end) portrays the behind-the-scenes work necessary to keep the political process moving.

Charlie Nye ends the story of his daughter's day of birth with a picture of his son holding the newborn while mother watches. The more than 19-hour story of a birth ends and the story of a new person, Abby Ruth Nye, begins.

Barbara F. Gundle's picture of a young man accepting the mantle of his religious duties and responsibilities at his Bar Mitzvah is another step in the life cycle—a coming of age.

The closing of a life cycle is depicted in Cynthia D. Stowell's portrait of a 91-year-old Indian woman at the Warm Springs Reservation. Past the age of active work, the woman accepts responsibility for caring for her grandchildren, passing on the wisdom and experience of her life.

As in any other state, people continue to earn their living at night. The 24-hour jobs in media, emergency services, entertainment and industry, all are necessary, because the demand for those positions exists. Other images in this section disclose police, farmers, disk jockeys, and even shipyard workers are active at night.

If the outsider is still showing signs of disbelief, take them on the statewide visual journey offered in this chapter. It should clinch the argument and show them that entertainment *is* thriving here.

Glimpses into the active centers of entertainment and nightlife include: Brent Wojahn's portrait of Carol Channing preparing for a

Portland performance of *Hello Dolly!,* or photographs by Steven Bloch of the after-theater crowd at the newly opened Metro on Broadway in Portland.

Night life in a smaller town is exemplified in Joel Davis's photograph of a ritual play-fight between regulars at a tavern in Pendleton, and Ross Hamilton's portrait of blues guitarist Terry Robb winding down a performance at a popular tavern in the countryside west of Portland.

As with the beginning of 15 July 1983, at the end of the day the same stars track over the skies of southeastern Oregon, persons sit in the Quality Pie shop in northwest Portland, and truckers and railroad men labor in the midst of another night of work. Yet, it is the beginning of the weekend, and many are those on their way to (or already arrived at) hideaways in the mountains, along the coast or even out of the state.

A new average day is about to be born; our *One Average Day* has come to a close.

204. HAMPTON STATION / 8:00 PM / DAVE SWAN

205. OAKRIDGE / 8:30 PM / VANESSA MCVAY

204. Motorcyclists Connie Whittington and Warner McMullen check their gear at Hampton Station on U. S. Highway 20, as the sun drops below the horizon.

205. Oakridge resident George Harrod lives on total disability due to several bypass operations, a pacemaker and back troubles. He uses his motorcycle and a long stick to gather bottles and cans for recycling, since he is unable to work. George says he has a lot more competition on the highway these days, young people picking up trash for the Highway Department.

204

205

116

206. EUGENE / 8:00 PM / AVERIE COHEN

207. FAIRVIEW / 6:45 PM / TOM TREICK

206. Two musicians take an evening break to exchange songs in a parking lot near the Eugene Amtrak station. Brenda Park was sitting alone outside ZooZoo's restaurant when Eagle Park Slim wandered over. He had been playing a benefit concert for El Salvador. He listened to her play, then picked up the guitar to offer her a song in return.

207. Before the first dog race starts, bettors discuss the racing forms at the Multnomah Kennel Club.

207

206

208.   Tim Sweek wrestles a surprised animal to the ground in the calf roping competition at The Dalles Rodeo.

208

209. The photographer's visit with Annie Yahtin is like a trip into another country and another century. Yahtin, 91, speaks only in the Sahaptin language; she is the third oldest person on the Warm Springs Reservation.

210. Actor Roby Robinson portrays an Indian, Coyote, in the Champoeg Historical Pageant. The pageant's program focuses on the formation of the state's first provisional government and the Oregon pioneers.

209

210

211. PORTLAND / 8:30 PM / BRYAN PETERSON

212. PORTLAND / 8:45 PM / BRYAN PETERSON

211. Dick Deegan is the foreman at Portland Shipyards and a member of the painter's union.

212. A welder at Portland Shipyards puts the finishing touches on a sonar detector for the bow of a ship.

211

212

ONE AVERAGE DAY

213. ALOHA / 9:00 PM / TERRY FARRIS

214. SPRINGFIELD / 9:00 PM / CHARLIE NYE

213. Ten-year-old Natalie Bortness receives a kiss from backstage director Lori Noyes at Mountain View Intermediate School. Bortness had just been crowned Little Miss Aloha, 1983.

214. Jeremy Nye watches his newborn sister Abby Ruth Nye while their mother watches at McKenzie-Willamette Hospital.

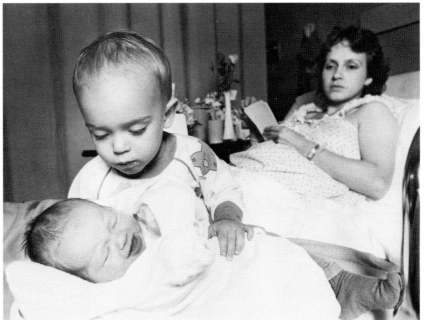

214

213

215. PORTLAND / 9:00 PM / BARBARA F. GUNDLE

216. PORTLAND / 7:35 PM / ROSS HAMILTON

217. PORTLAND / 2:40 PM / PAUL ENGSTROM

215. Brent Weil passes through his Bar Mitzvah, an initiation ceremony welcoming the young man to his religious duties and responsibilities, in the Havurah Shalom Synagogue at Southwest Portland's Jewish Community Center.

216. Eldridge L. Cleaver, author and black activist, gives a sermon at the Northwest Service Center.

217. In an interview earlier in the afternoon with a reporter for the *Oregonian,* Eldridge L. Cleaver discusses his conversion to Christianity. The former Black Panther leader and author of *Soul on Ice* is now a Christian activist.

215

216

217

218. Carol Channing prepares for an evening performance of *Hello, Dolly!* at Portland's Civic Auditorium.

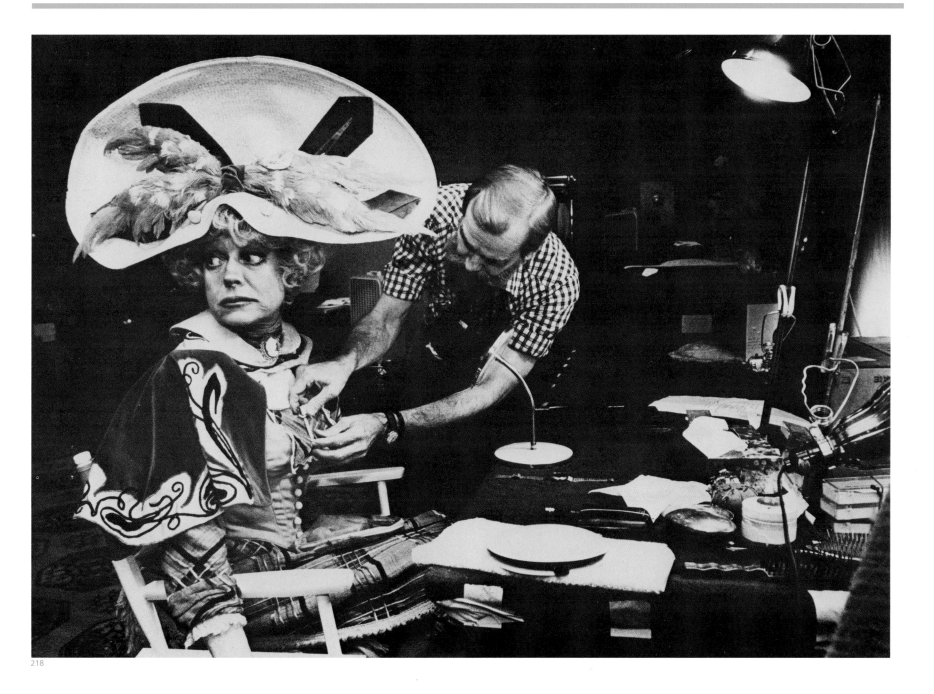

218

219. PORTLAND / 10:00 PM / PAUL ENGSTROM

220. PORTLAND / 10:20 PM / STEVE BLOCH

221. PORTLAND / 11:30 PM / PAUL ENGSTROM

219. Nightlife in Portland. The Storefront Theatre is well-known for offering contemporary productions to the theatre-going crowd of Oregon's largest city.

220. Outside of McDonald's, near the Galleria in downtown Portland, an evening stroller stops to light up a cigarette.

221. "Mother Louise," the reigning Miss Gay Portland is en route to the Dahl and Penne Tavern, where Mother Louise is performing in a drag show.

222.   PENDLETON / 10:00 PM / ROBERT
PENNELL

223.   PENDLETON / 10:00 PM / ROBERT
PENNELL

222.   Two tavern regulars at Hat's Elkhorn
Tavern in Pendleton carry out a friendly
sparring ritual as their evening begins.

223.   The sparring is good-natured. Hat's
Elkhorn Tavern is one of the few predomi-
nantly Indian taverns in Pendleton.

222

223

224. LAKEVIEW / 11:15 PM / J.L. CLARK

225. WARM SPRINGS RESERVATION / 10:30 PM / CYNTHIA D. STOWELL

224. A Lakeview farmer bales hay throughout the night, "while the weather is good." This year's excessive wet weather set back schedules of many Oregon farmers.

225. A swing shift sawfitter, Emerson "Chief" Smith, at Warm Springs Forest Products Industries, replaces a dull blade. While the rest of the millworkers take breaks, he hoists band saws and gang saws through holes in the floor and replaces them with sharpened blades. He also checks the teeth and flat surfaces of the band saws as they are automatically filed. As soon as his shift ends, the sawfitter plans to go to a rodeo in Fallon, Nevada.

224

225

226. SALEM / 10:30 PM / MICHAEL LLOYD

227. PORTLAND / 10:00 PM / CLAUDIA J. HOWELL

226. It is a never-ending day for lobbyists and policemen. A lobbyist places a last-minute call in Salem while the legislature continues into the night.

227. In north Portland, a policeman stops a motorist to warn him that his taillights are not working. No ticket was given.

226

227

228.   PORTLAND / 11:00 PM / STEVE
BLOCH

229.   PORTLAND / 11:15 PM / STEVE
BLOCH

228.   A regular of the Metro on Broadway (where Portland's New Wave elite exchange information on bands and friends and the social scene) takes a pensive smoke.

229.   An employee of Ears to You at the Metro on Broadway in downtown Portland keeps his eyes on the action in this moody photograph.

228

229

230. PORTLAND / 11:10 PM / STEVE
BLOCH

231. PORTLAND / 11:50 PM / STEVE
BLOCH

230. Ordering espresso coffee at the
height of the evening rush at one of the
five featured restaurants of the Metro on
Broadway.

231. Playful and pretty, a customer settles
in at a table with her coffee near the
Broadway street entrance of the Metro on
Broadway.

230

231

232. ROSEBURG / 11:49 PM / LISA STONE

232. Disk jockey Annie Mac slides into the last 11 minutes of her evening shift with a news tape — and hot java for herself.

232

233. ROCK CREEK / 11:55 PM / ROSS
HAMILTON

233.   Terry Robb, leader of the Terry Robb
Band, a rock and blues group, concentrates
during a performance at Washington
County's Rock Creek Tavern.

233

GOVERNOR'S PROCLAMATION

VICTOR ATIYEH
GOVERNOR

OFFICE OF THE GOVERNOR
STATE CAPITOL
SALEM OREGON 97310

July 8, 1983

STATEMENT BY GOVERNOR VIC ATIYEH

Over 70 photojournalists will be documenting one average day in the history of Oregon on July 15, 1983. The 24-hour project includes regional and nationally known photographers who have volunteered their time to capture the essense of daily life in Oregon within the broad themes of The Land, The People, The Work, and The Pastimes. Within the specified 24-hour period each photographer will donate that day's work in the form of prints to the collection.

Images collected through Project Dayshoot will be placed in the Oregon Historical Society archives. The collection will be displayed in a 200-page book produced by the society, and in an exhibit at the society's gallery which is scheduled for March of 1984.

The products of Project Dayshoot will provide an insight and reference of contemporary Oregon for future generations of Oregonians.

Therefore, as Governor, I hereby proclaim July 15, 1983, as

"OREGON PHOTOJOURNALISM DAY"

and call upon all Oregonians to recognize the many contributions that photojournalists are making to preserve the daily elements of our lives.

Victor Atiyeh
Governor

COLOPHON

One Average Day is typeset in a Mergenthaler version of Frutiger. Frutiger is a recent design by one of the foremost contemporary typographic artists, Adrian Frutiger.

Born in Switzerland in 1928, Frutiger was chosen in his early twenties as the artistic director of the largest French typecasting and type design firm, Deberny and Peignot. Frutiger soon gained world-wide fame for his family of san serif type known as Univers, which was first introduced in 1957. Meridien and other popular faces also have come from his creative mind, and he successfully completed the formidable task of producing a readable Devanagari type for use in the modern Indian languages associated with Hindi.

The san serif named for Frutiger used in *One Average Day* is based on a commission to design the signage at Charles deGaulle Airport in Paris. It was officially introduced in 1975-76. It is a clean, fine example of the best of san serif designs, and has special qualities in its short curves of the capital C and S and a capital G that has no spur. Frutiger was chosen for *One Average Day* because it has clean, modern, san serif qualities, qualities that mesh well with photographs.

All the black-and-white images are reproduced in 175-line screen duotones, black with a second color gray (PMS 407). The four-color reproductions have the same screen value. The typography throughout the book, except on the double-page openings of the six chapters, is printed in the gray, as are the painted pages at the beginning of each chapter.

One Average Day was designed and produced by Western Imprints, The Press of the Oregon Historical Society.

The firms involved in the book's production:

Typesetter:	Paul O. Giesey/Adcrafters
Color separator:	Trade Litho
Paper suppliers:	Western Paper
	Text (80lb. Wedgewood Gloss)
	Paperbound cover (.012pt. Kromekote)
	Carpenter-Offutt
	Endpaper (50lb. Quality Cover, antique finish)
	James River Graphics
	Clothbound cover (Kivar 6, chrome finish)
Printer:	Schultz / Wack / Weir
Binder:	Lincoln & Allen